Journal of the
INDIAN WARS

Volume Two, No. 1

Carnelian Publishing Company

P.O. Box 4527, El Dorado Hills, CA 95762

Subscription and Publishing Information

Journal of the Indian Wars (*JIW*) is published quarterly by Carnelian Publishing Company, P.O. Box 4527, El Dorado Hills, CA 95762. Publisher: Theodore P. Savas. (916) 941-6896 (voice); (916)-941-6895 (fax); e-mail: militarybooks@onemain.com. Our online military history catalog of original books is found at www.savaspublishing.com and /or www.Carnelianpublishing.com.

SUBSCRIPTIONS to *JIW* are available at $29.95/yr. (four books); Canada and overseas is $39.95/yr., surface mail. Write to: Carnelian Publishing Company, *JIW* Subscriptions, P.O. Box 4527, El Dorado Hills, CA 95762. Check, MO, MC or V accepted. Phone, fax or e-mail orders welcome. All subscriptions begin with the current issue unless otherwise specified.

DISTRIBUTION in North America is handled by Stackpole Books, 5067 Ritter Road, Mechanicsburg, PA 17055-6921. 800-732-3669 (voice); 717-976-0412 (fax); E-mail: prossi@stackpolebooks.com. Back issues of *JIW* are available. Retail price for each is $11.95 plus shipping ($3.00 for the first book and $1.00 for each additional book). Inquire as to availability. Check, money order, MC/V, AE, or D are accepted. Contact Stackpole Books for quantity discounts.

MANUSCRIPTS, REVIEWS, AND NEWS SUBMISSIONS are welcome. For guidelines, consult our web site (www.savaspublishing.com and /or www.carnelianpublishing.com), or send a self-addressed stamped envelope to Michael A. Hughes, Editor, *Journal of the Indian Wars*, 1317 S Cherry, Ada, OK 74820-8137. Proposals for articles (recommended) should include a brief description of your topic, a list of primary sources, and estimate of completion date. Manuscripts should be accompanied by a 3.5" disk with copies in both WordPerfect 5 or 6.1, Word, and/or Rich Text (RTF) formats. Persons interested in reviewing books should send a description of their qualifications, areas of expertise, and desired titles and topics. News submissions should include a brief abstracted version of any information. Submitted news may be posted on our web site at our discretion. Enclose a SASE if requesting a reply and include your e-mail and fax number. Publications (which may include page proofs) and videos for potential review should be sent to the managing editor.

Carnelian Publishing Company expressly disclaims all responsibility for statements, whether of opinion or fact, contained herein.

JIW is published with the cooperation of Jerry Russell and the Order of the Indian Wars. Without Jerry's none-too-gentle proddings and earnest supplications, it would not have come to fruition. For more information, please write to OIW, P.O. Box 7401, Little Rock AR 72217.

Journal of the Indian Wars, Vol. Two, No. 1,
ISBN: 1-882810-88-0 Copyright © 2001 Theodore P. Savas
All rights not reverting to contributors reserved; protected under the Berne Convention

Carnelian Publishing Company

Publisher
Theodore P. Savas

Editorial Assistants: Patrick A. Bowmaster, William Haley
Graphics: James Zach
Marketing: Carol A. Savas
Indexing: Lee W. Merideth

Journal of the Indian Wars

Managing Editor: Michael A. Hughes
Associate Editors: Patrick A. Bowmaster, Rod Thomas,
Phil Konstantin, and Eril B. Hughes
Book Review Editor: Patrick Jung
Advertising/Circulation: Carol A. Savas
Editorial Consultants: Brian Pohanka,
Jerry Keenan, Neil Mangum, Jerry Russell, and Ted Alexander

Civil War Regiments Journal

Managing Editor: Theodore P. Savas

Assistant Editors: Lee Merideth, William Haley
Circulation/Advertising: Carol Savas
Book Review Editor: Archie McDonald

Cover Images
Courtesy of the various displayed

Contributors

Sandy Barnard, a journalist and founder of AST Press, is the author of *Digging Into Custer's Last Stand* and *Custer's First Sergeant, John Ryan*. He was media director for several archeological surveys of the Little Bighorn Battlefield and is editor of the Custer Battlefield Historical and Museum Association's *Greasy Grass* research annual.

Colin G. Calloway is a professor of history at Dartmouth College and a prolific author and editor of American Indian historiography and New England Indian history. His best known books include *The American Revolution in Indian Country*; *Crown and Calumet: British-Indian Relations, 1783-1815*; and two works on the Abenakis.

Patrick Jung is an adjunct professor of history and an administrator at Marquette University. He is also the book review editor of this journal. His primary areas of research include the history of the Great Lakes and Ohio River basin regions and the late colonial and early national periods of United States history.

Rodney G. Thomas retired as a colonel from the U.S. Army in 1999 but has worked full time since as a corporate consultant. He is an associate editor of this journal and maintains and advises on web sites for organizations such as Little Big Horn Association.

Clifford E. Trafzer is a professor of history and Native American studies at the University of California, Riverside. He is the author of a wide range of books and articles, many of them on the Indian nations of California and the Pacific Northwest. Among his best known works are *Exterminate Them*; *The Kit Carson Campaign*; and *Renegade Tribe: The Palouse Indians and the Invasion of the Inland Pacific Northwest*.

Journal of the INDIAN WARS
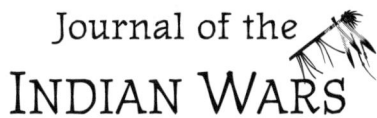

Table of Contents

Foreword   I

Book Commentaries I: The Art of Research   1

Beyond Body Counts: Search for Multiple Meanings of Conflict in Indian Wars   9
Colin G. Calloway

Book Commentaries II: The East and Pre-Nineteenth Century Wars   14

The Works of Rev. Francis Paul Prucha, S.J.   25
Patrick Jung

Book Commentaries III: Camp, Custer, and the Little Bighorn   29

Walter Mason Camp: My Favorite Researcher of the Little Bighorn   42
Sandy Barnard

Ten Essential Books for Understanding the Battle of the Little Bighorn   51
JIW Staff

continued

Table of Contents (continued)

Book Commentaries IV: The Rest of the West   55

Native Voices: There are no Accidents   70
Clifford E. Trafzer

By Glint of Lantern Late:
The Texts of Custer and the Cadets   73
Rodney Thomas

Suggested Readings on the
Fifteen Greatest Indian Wars   81
JIW Staff

A Conversation with
the Late Terry Johnston   105
Interviewed by Michael A. Hughes

The Indian Wars: Organizational,
Tribal, and Museum News   115

Book Reviews   125

Foreword

Michael A. Hughes, editor

Nobelist William Faulkner once said that the past isn't dead, it isn't even past. Though Faulkner had the history of the United States's "Old South" in mind, his sentiment would seem equally true of Indian wars history. This year of 2001 is the one hundredth anniversary of what some consider the last "Indian uprising" in the United States. The event, in 1901, was a militant protest by Chitto Harjo's Muskogee Creek traditionalists against the Dawe's Act, which parceled off the Indian reservations. Today, when I pick up the local phone directory in our Oklahoma office and note its eighteen listings for Harjos, the past indeed seems very much alive.

Reaching the second volume of any privately funded scholarly journal is a milestone, and we have reached it. We thank our many readers, contributors, and advisors who have helped us achieve this goal. To celebrate the occasion, this issue is about . . . publications. More precisely, this issue is about books and authors dealing with the Indian wars. In preparation for this special issue, we spent more than six months asking notable authors, publishers, and bibliophiles about significant Indian wars-related books. The query process was informal and certainly not every authority in the field was contacted. Those queried were asked to identify their favorite books on the subject, or at least which books and authors most impressed and inspired them. Authors were also invited to explain how they came to write the book for which they are best known.

The "guardian saint" of *JIW*, advisory board member Jerry Keenan, was the first to reply. His highly appropriate choice was a commentary on the work of the "dean" of western Indian wars historians, Robert M. Utley. When Utley likewise penned a comment, his prestige was such that it encouraged many others to participate. As will be seen, dozens of individuals were kind enough to send a paragraph or two in response to our letters and e-mail messages. Some of the busiest and most highly respected authors went so far as to contribute entire essays. Canadian scholars were particularly gracious, with almost every researcher of that country that we contacted providing a response. This issue also includes a variety of articles and essays relative to research and publication we are confident our readers will find of interest.

But it has not been a smooth road. Both the publisher and the managing editor have recently moved to more historic locations. The book publishing portion of Savas Publishing Company was recently acquired by Combined Publishing of Conshohocken, Pennsylvania, with acquisitions editing headquarters moving from Iowa to famed El Dorado County, California, the site of the famed 1848 California gold strike. Copyright and inventory issues snarled production to a disquieting halt for months. While the publisher dealt with that nightmare, the editorial office for *JIW* moved across the town of Ada, Oklahoma. We are now located on the crest of Delaware Mount, an elevation once used by outriders of the "Delaware" or Lennai Lenape Indians to scout for bison. What is now the drive at the end of the block was once the California Road, a path blazed across the Choctaw and Chickasaw nations by prospectors and military engineers during the California Gold Rush.

Unfortunately, relocating to our respective new addresses unleashed some variety of arcane curse. We have been struck with three separate ice storms and wind storms, and numerous random power, telephone, and computer outages. To date we have been deprived of an ancient elm tree, part of the rear wall of our office, two telephone lines, two computer hard drives, and an undetermined number of computer files. Electricity has been lost six times, phone service eight, , and tempers several times that count. We are now on a first name basis with three carpenters and electricians, two Southwestern Bell linemen, two Apple sales representatives, a MacIntosh computer technician, and a tree surgeon. Anyone on a first-name basis with a Lenape shaman and an army chaplain is invited to introduce them to us, just in case.

Finally, associate editor Rod Thomas and I enjoyed very much celebrating the 125th anniversary of the Little Bighorn with many of our readers this past June.

BOOK COMMENTARIES
Research and Discovery

Frank Laumer, author of *Dade's Last Battle* and *Amidst a Storm of Bullets: The Diary of Lt. Henry Prince in Florida, 1832-1842*, on discovering the diary of Lieutenant Prince.

Finding a Needle. A needle is no easier to find in the haystack of history than in an actual stack of hay. It takes more luck than skill. In my case, it was entirely luck.

My home is on the north bank of the Withlacoochee River in Florida, half a mile west of Fort Dade, fifty miles north of Ft. Brooke (Tampa). Thirteen miles farther on by the Ft. King Road lies Dade Battlefield State Historic Site. For fifteen years I had been doing research and writing on every detail relating to this bloody engagement between Seminole Indians and American soldiers. On the 29th of October, 1978, I received a telephone call from Winnie Murphy, museum guide at the Battlefield. A visiting couple claimed to own a diary written during the years 1836 through 1842 by an officer of the United States Army stationed in Florida during that period. The diary allegedly included maps, sketches of Seminole War forts, even a drawing of Dade Battlefield itself done only weeks after the battle. I immediately invited the couple to visit me.

Ralph Coggeshall was a tall, well-spoken man, perhaps sixty years old. I asked him first the name of the diarist, afraid that my hope for a new view of the Second Seminole War period would be ended by the name Cohen, Potter, Duncan, Bemrose, or another known writer of the period. "Lt. Henry Prince," Mr. Coggeshall replied. Prince? Who in the world was Henry Prince? Certainly no one that I had come across in several years of research. Had I understood correctly that what he had was an original diary, not a photocopy, photostat, typescript?

Yes, the diary was in longhand, several hundred pages, mostly in ink, some in pencil. Small handwriting, but generally quite legible. Small pages, perhaps four or five inches square, loose. A great many maps of the military roads, sketches of Ft. Brooke, Ft. Foster, that sort of thing. I asked how he had come by this diary.

"It was found in a trunk in the attic of the home of Dr. C. A. Van Slyke by his daughter, my wife (Lucille M. Van Slyke), following his death in 1940. The Van Slyke family were pioneers from Cooperstown, New York, who settled in St. Paul, Minnesota, in 1854. Our guess is that Prince was a friend of someone in the Van Slyke family," Mr. Coggeshall continued, "and left the diary with them for safekeeping while he was away with the army during the Civil War. He probably just neglected to come back for it."

I asked if Mr. Coggeshall and his wife would consider selling the diary in order for it to be brought back to Florida and made available to researchers. Well, they would think about it. They were in Florida on vacation from their home in New Jersey and would be returning there within a few weeks. They would let me know. During November and December, I talked to Mr. Coggeshall a number of times on the phone, and we exchanged several letters. He sent me a sample of a dozen or so photocopied pages of the diary.

I was distressed to see that someone, perhaps in an effort to clarify occasional dates and names, had made bold emendations with a ball-point pen here and there across the faint original writing. It was unfortunate, but not a serious threat to the integrity of the work. A typical page contained 36 lines of handwriting, averaging eight words to the line, a total of 288 words per page. If there were even 100 pages of text it would mean nearly 30,000 words of a West Point, eyewitness account of the Second Seminole War, the longest, bloodiest and most costly war with Native Americans in United States history. Words unknown to the field of Florida history.

On December, 17, 1978, Mr. Coggeshall wrote that he and his wife had decided to offer the diary for sale. On the 9th of January, my wife Dale Anne, our two small daughters (Amie and Jodi), and I arrived at the Coggeshall home. Coggeshall brought out a packet of paper perhaps an inch and a half thick and set it before me. The diary. Winter sunlight seemed to glow on the little pile of paper. I touched it, turned back a paper cover. I read "1836—Land of Flowers. Aim to 'gather laurels'. January 10." Tomorrow it would be exactly 142 years since Henry Prince, 2nd Lieutenant, 4th Regiment Infantry, U.S. Army, had written these opening words at St. Augustine, Florida. I turned more pages and caught glimpses of places, men, battles. Here was no dry, indifferent account of nameless places, faceless men, battles reckoned only by whether they were won or lost. Here was life, color, detail. It was apparent that Henry Prince had been a participant in, as well as an interested observer of, the events through which the land of the Seminoles had been taken from them, blacks returned to slavery, thousands of lives lost, Florida set on the road that would transform it from a battleground into a nation's playground. Needle indeed.

Henry Prince had met many of the leading participants during the tragic drama of the Second Seminole War: Osceola, Micanopy, Zachary Taylor, Clinch, Gaines, Dade. Prince had designed Ft. Foster, described by his commanding officer as "one of the strongest and best field fortifications ever erected (against Indians) on this continent." A drawing of the fort filled an entire page. Prince had mapped the course of the Withlacoochee River from Ft. Dade to Ft. Cooper. From the window of the tower where I write, I would have seen him pass. He wrote of swimming in these same dark and lovely waters that still hurry past my home. He had quartered at Ft. Dade, traveled up and down the Ft. King Road, visited and sketched the graves of Dade's command when the graves were new. He had visited Powel's (Osceola's) Town, the now legendary refuge of the Indian leader in the "Cove of the Withlacoochee" and described it in minute detail. He had traveled Florida from the Atlantic to the Gulf, from Georgia to Key West. And all that he experienced he described—sometimes briefly as circumstances of battle or march allowed, sometimes with vivid simile: "the bullets twitter over our heads like a rush of blackbirds" (during Gaines's battle at the Withlacoochee, 5 March 1836). This young officer who "aimed to gather laurels" had gathered wounds instead.

Mr. Coggeshall was as concerned as I that the diary return to Florida and be available for research. He named a modest price; I wrote a check.

Twenty years later, through letters and phone calls, travel here and abroad, and with the help of a great many people, I discovered quite a lot about the life of Henry Prince. His diary is the only extended record known to exist written in the field during the Second Seminole War. Research and editing finally done, publication of this extraordinary document was funded by the Seminole Wars Historic Foundation, Inc., through the University of Tampa Press.

"How I would delight to have the world see the exciting panorama of events, acts, and pictures that I have seen," wrote Henry Prince. Now it can.

Olive Dickason, professor emeritus, University of Alberta, and adjunct professor, University of Ottawa, on writing *The Myth of the Savage and the Beginnings of French Colonialism in the Americas* and *Canada's First Nations: A History of Founding Peoples from Earliest Time*s (winner of the Sir John A. McDonald Prize from the Canadian Historical Association).

When I returned to university as a history student after twenty-four years in journalism, I was unpleasantly surprised to find old attitudes about "savages" firmly entrenched in academia. Soon realizing that if I felt as strongly about honoring all my ancestors as I thought I did, then it was

up to me to do the work necessary to demonstrate the error of those stereotypes. That led to another problem—the prevalent belief that Indians had no history. Since they did not possess writing, how could they? In historical studies, as in the law courts at that time, oral tradition was given no more weight than gossip. It was my good fortune that a sympathetic professor took up my cause, and I was eventually able to pursue the researches that led to my book, *The Myth of the Savage*, and later, to *Canada's First Nations*.

John D. McDermott, researcher and author of *Forlorn Hope: The Battle of White Bird Canyon and the Beginning of the Nez Perce War* and *A Guide to the Indian Wars of the West*, on his favorite Indian wars source.

If I had my way, I would spend the rest of my days reading nineteenth century newspapers, for it is there that you find the human stories and the varied viewpoints that make the Indian wars fascinating. One of the most interesting compendiums is the *National Tribune*, the Washington, D. C.-published paper that was the official organ of the Grand Old Army of the Republic in its early years, and, after 1890, a treasure trove of reminiscences, diary excerpts, and articles from the pens of Indian wars veterans. Enough of officers' obfuscation and commanders' cover-ups! Here is the meat of history, where we learn about man's frailties and cruelties, what he thought, and what he did.

Take, for example, Patrick Connor's attack on an Arapaho camp on Tongue River on August 29, 1865. Two enlisted men wrote about it in the *National Tribune* on February 11, 1898, and June 9, 1910. The first was Charles W. Adams of Company K, Eleventh Ohio Volunteer Cavalry. In his reminiscence, Adams described the scene of the attack: "The bugle sounded forward and away we went. As we neared the village the command divided, some turning to the right, others to the left. . . . The Indians had some of their tepees down and ponies packed, and some were so heavily laden that when they tried to run the packs pulled them over and they lay with their feet in the air." The picture of the overburdened ponies with their feet in the air makes the scene come alive and says much about the grasping nature of man, even in times of extreme danger.

The other participant, Private P. W. Brown, described the bizarre wound experienced by another soldier: "I remember Comrade Johnson, our company, who was shot, the arrow going thru. [sic] his cheek and tongue, and fastening itself in the jawbone, where it remained until we arrived back at camp, where the Doctor and another man were required to get it out." Brown reminds us that these were times when weapons were primitive and the results unpredictable—and often messy.

And it is in the newspapers where we find the details that recreate the feelings accompanying an event. George Webber of the Twenty-seventh Infantry wrote in the *National Tribune* in 1897 about the aftermath of the Fetterman Fight in late December, 1866:

"The dead were deposited in the spare ward of the hospital, two hospital tents and double cabin. Details from each company assisted in their care and identification. Many gave their best uniforms to clothe decently their comrades, and the good traits of the solder were touchingly discussed as mutilated fragments were carefully handled, arrows drawn or cut out and the remains composed for the burial. A long line of pine cases, duly numbered, was arranged by companies along the officers' street near the hospital, and as each was placed in its plain receptacle the number and name was taken for the future reference of friends. The detail to dig a grave for its great entombment was well armed and accompanied by a guard, but so intense was the cold that constant relays were required. Over the great pit, fifty feet long and seven feet deep, a mound was raised. Then the ceremonies were performed."

These are the stories that count and remind us that the Indian wars were not a game but a deadly business of suffering, injury, and death to the unlucky.

Father Barry Hagan, C.S.C., University of Portland, on writing *Exactly in the Right Place: A History of Fort C. F. Smith, Montana Territory, 1866-1868*.

I was summer vacationing in Glendive, Montana, my home town, when I accidentally came across *Fort Phil Kearny*, later retitled The *Fetterman Massacre*, by Dee Brown. From his book I first learned of the existence and story of Forts Phil Kearny and Reno, both in Wyoming, and C. F. Smith in Montana, perhaps 150 miles from my hometown. And I learned of the Bozeman Trail, which wound through both of those states. Soon I read *Ab-sa-ra-ka* and *My Army Life* by the two [Col. Henry B.] Carrington wives, which cover the first 25 percent of Fort Phil Kearny's brief existence.

I wanted to write a book covering the entire history of all three of these forts. And so I hired a graduate student with a master's in history to go to the National Archives in Washington, D.C., and get copies of the relevant documents. He spent four months, six days a week, eight hours a day, in that building, which was then without air conditioning. From Washington came boxes of photocopies of these documents. Because I am legally blind, I hired a full-time secretary to go through the reams of material. Then, she and the graduate student poured through more than fifty reels of microfilm of records and old newspapers.

Each of these three forts was a community with a sizeable number of army personnel and civilian employees. Then there were the Sioux, who were at the forts attacking the stockades or freight trains, and the sizeable number of civilians going to and from Virginia City, Montana. We began to make sense of the records, diaries, letters to newspapers, and letters home. It gradually became evident that a complete history from sources existed for only Fort C. F. Smith, with perhaps 25 percent of the sources needed for Fort Kearny and 10 percent of the sources needed for Fort Reno. I wrote three book length manuscripts, each successively shorter than the last, as I drew upon sources from more than thirteen archives. My book, *Exactly in the Right Place: A History of Fort C. F. Smith*, was published by Upton and Sons of El Segundo, California. And more then fifteen boxes of source material, everything I had collected, was accepted by and housed in the Wyoming Room of the Fulmer Public Library in Sheridan, Wyoming, where it is open to the public, as are all of the finding aids concerned with them.

Book Commentaries: Research and Discovery 7

Louis Kraft, author of *Custer and the Cheyenne* and *Gatewood and Geronimo*, on research in the Charles Gatewood collection in Arizona.

Unbelievable as it may seem, a film that dealt with the end of the Apache wars (*Geronimo: An American Legend*) has become the focal point for my writing projects. I saw it when it opened at the end of 1993, and although I liked its majesty and harshness, I was bothered that there was no central focus to draw me into the story. Without bothering to check its accuracy, I quickly forgot about it.

Two years later I visited Guidon Books (Scottsdale, Arizona) to publicize *Custer and the Cheyenne* (Upton and Sons, 1995). The conversation with Ruth and Aaron Cohen (proprietors of Guidon) turned to films and how they affect book sales. Surprisingly, Ruth (who died in 1999) said that *Geronimo: An American Legend* had not helped sales at all. This set off a conversation on one of the characters in the film, Lieutenant Charles Gatewood (Sixth U.S. Cavalry). I knew nothing about him except what I had seen in the movie. The talk turned to the Gatewood Collection, housed at the Arizona Historical Society in Tucson. As little had been written about him, I decided to check out the collection the following month. The exploratory trip to Tucson quickly made me realize that even though the film presented its action in a way that made it appear to be truthful, it was actually off on just about everything. For example, in the film Lieutenant Britton Davis (Fourth U.S. Cavalry), Chiricahua warrior-turned-scout Chatto, and chief of scouts, Al Sieber, accompany Gatewood into the wilds of Mexico in 1886 to find Geronimo and talk him into returning to the United States to surrender. Unfortunately, none of them were with Gatewood during the mission. In fact, Davis (who is the narrator of the film) had already resigned from the army. More important than realizing that the film was typical of Hollywood's efforts of turning fact into fiction, however, was that I had found an exceptional man. The hunt was on.

Gatewood's background stemmed from his Southern-bred feelings of superiority to other races and the newfound hatreds created by the tyranny of the aftermath of the Civil War. He was both a commander of Apache scouts and military commandant of the White Mountain Indian Reservation (headquartered at Fort Apache, Arizona). His upbringing did not taint his treatment of Native Americans. In fact, his stance for their rights constantly placed him at odds with both his superiors and the citizens of Arizona. The

Apaches looked upon Gatewood as one of only a handful of white men who dealt with them fairly.

Although my research culminated with the publication of *Gatewood & Geronimo* (University of New Mexico Press, 2000), my connection with the Apaches and Gatewood has not ended. What began as a simple viewing of *Geronimo: An American Legend* in 1993 has resulted in my writing career traveling a path I never anticipated. I am currently working on a second Gatewood project that is due at the University of New Mexico Press in 2001. In all likelihood, others will follow.

BEYOND BODY COUNTS

Searching for the Multiple Meanings of Conflict in Indian Wars.

Colin G. Calloway

Historical documents do not always provide an accurate and unbiased record of what actually happened, and military records may be the most suspect of all. Soldiers on different sides might remember events very differently; accounts of events recalled after the heat of battle and tallies of casualties inflicted on enemies beyond the smoke or the trees are likely to be inaccurate, and officers' reports may be more concerned with justifying conduct than conveying full and precise information. The problems are compounded when conflicts involved Euro-Americans and Native Americans. Indian peoples lived in an oral culture; warriors recounted their deeds in battle, and people knew their military record and reputation, but rarely did Indians produce written accounts of the wars they fought. Europeans who fought on different sides generally shared a common understanding of what they were doing when they went into battle, but Indians often had very different understandings of the meanings, purposes, and practice of war, and different notions of what constituted victory and defeat. Historians who aspire to achieve a balanced narrative of Indian-white conflict face a daunting task in doing justice to encounters that were as much a conflict of world views as they were a clash of armies.

Good history, of course, demands consulting all sources available. Doing Indian history requiresincluding oral traditions in those sources. Historians who are trained to use the written word are often distrustful of oral sources, but documents are not always to be trusted either. They do not convey the "truth" of what happened; they only convey what their authors thought, wanted to think, or wanted others to think happened. Oral traditions can prompt searching questions of the accounts presented in written records and can also serve as an important complement to written history. Many years ago, linguist, ethnologist and ethno-historian Gordon M. Day recorded an Abenaki tradition that told how most of the Abenaki people living at the village of Odanak or St. Francis in Quebec escaped the attack launched by Robert Rogers and his Rangers in 1759 (an assault fictionalized in the Kenneth Robert's novel and Spencer Tracy movie, *Northwest Passage*).

According to the Abenaki tradition, one of Rogers's Indian scouts warned the inhabitants of the village and most of the people went into hiding.1 The account seems implausible if one accepts without question Robert Rogers's own published account, which is the only primary document in English. In Rogers's version, the Rangers caught the Abenakis by surprise, killed two hundred Indians, and destroyed the village. But Rogers, who had little opportunity to conduct an accurate body count, had to justify a campaign in which he lost a third of his command. The French in Quebec, who were allies of the Abenakis and much closer to them, had less reason to tamper with the figures. The French reckoned the Rangers killed only about thirty Indians, not the two hundred of which Rogers boasted, and Abenakis from Odanak were raiding the New England frontier again the next year.2 Weighing the English, French, and Indian evidence together suggests that an oral tradition passed with care from generation to generation may have more validity and reliability than a document written to enhance or protect a commander's reputation.

Indian oral history helps to clarify events in another famous battle, 109 years later and 2,000 miles to the west. On the night of June 26, 1876, survivors of Major Marcus Reno's battalion were pinned down on a hill overlooking the Little Bighorn River, after the Seventh Cavalry's disastrous attack that day on the Lakota and Cheyenne village there. Though the encircled troops did not know it yet, George Armstrong Custer had been wiped out with his entire command at the north end of the village. As Reno's men looked down on the village that night, they heard the Indians drumming and singing in "wild victory dances." The soldiers expected to die the next morning. But the accounts written by the soldiers on the scene were incorrect interpretations. Indians in the village who were interviewed in old age said that what the soldiers heard were not victory dances, but mourning songs for the men who had died in the fighting. The Indians packed up their village and moved off. Reno's men survived.[3]

Native American accounts can also complicate our understanding of what battles meant to various participants. Indians and whites employed different strategies but also often had very different concepts of war. Plains Indian ledger art—drawings done in the late nineteenth century on pages torn from account books—depicted individual warriors winning war honors against disciplined soldiers fighting in formation. Indian actions in battle often made little sense to Europeans and Americans, but Indian accounts reveal that a conflict such as the Battle of the Little Bighorn, which has been closely analyzed by military historians, was fought on many levels, and was experienced and understood in different ways.[4]

In early conflicts, it was not unusual for Europeans as well as Indians to regard war as a spiritual as well as a military endeavor. Spanish conquistadors yelled "Santiago!" [Saint James] as they spurred into battle and believed that St. James accompanied them. According to some accounts, the Indians later asserted that when Spanish troops stormed and captured the mesa stronghold of the Acoma Pueblos in New Mexico in 1599, the defenders in the heat of the battle had seen someone on a white horse, dressed in white, a red emblem on his breast, and spear in his hand. As a biography of conqueror Don Juan de Oñate notes, "The Spaniards believed that without special aid from our God it would have been impossible to gain such a victory."[5] Europeans would later put more faith in keeping their powder dry than in God, but for Indians war remained a sacred contest. Indian warriors in old age recited life stories dominated by the quest for visions and powerful medicine as the key to success in war.[6]

In the eastern woodlands, fewer Indian accounts survive of their experiences in battle and their understandings of war. But sources written by their European adversaries can provide glimpses and clues. What, for example, are we to make of the fact that as Hernando De Soto's army of Spanish conquistadors advanced through the Southeast, Indian warriors on occasion abandoned their villages and left their women and children behind? Were they cowards who fled without a thought for their families? The fact that they returned to harass the invaders suggests not. Did they instead perhaps assume that the non-combatants would be safe, since in their experience warriors did not kill women and children? Almost a hundred years later, in New England, Pequot warriors asked English soldiers if they killed women and children.[7] The English gave their answer when they massacred hundreds of Pequots in their burning village on the Mystic River in 1637. That action may not have seemed extreme to European eyes at a time when the Thirty Years War was ravaging Europe, but the Pequot question implies some different notions of warfare. Indians did not understand the systematic destruction of corn fields or buffalo herds as instruments of war; Euro-Americans did not understand warriors' pursuit of individual honor even as their people were being starved into submission.

Narratives of Indian-white warfare are woven into the fabric of American history, and they dominate our understandings of Native American history. But most of them, often by necessity, provide only a partial reconstruction of conflicts waged by different societies for different purposes and in confusing circumstances. As Inga Clendinnen demonstrated in her masterful examination of the clash of Aztec and Spanish warrior societies, how people wage war and what they understand by that war can reveal much about their values and view of their place in the world.[8] The so-called "Indian wars" were not just military encounters; they were a clash of cultures that sometimes revealed different understandings of humanity. They can, if scrutinized closely, provide important glimpses into the worlds of people who too often feature as little more than head counts or body counts in our histories of conflict in America.

NOTES

1. Gordon M. Day, "Rogers' Raid in Indian Tradition," *Historical New Hampshire* 17 (June 1962), 3-17; idem., "Oral Tradition as Complement," *Ethnohistory* 19 (1972), 99-108.

2. Colin G. Calloway, *The Western Abenakis of Vermont: War, Migration, and the Survival of an Indian People, 1600-1800* (Norman: University of Oklahoma Press, 1990), 177-179.

3. James Welch and Paul Stekler, *Killing Custer: The Battle of the Little Big Horn and the Fate of the Plains Indians* (New York: W. W. Norton, 1994), 287-289, 295.

4. See, for example, Richard G. Hardorff, comp. and ed., *Lakota Recollections of the Custer Fight: New Sources of Indian-Military History* (1991; Lincoln: University of Nebraska Press, 1997); idem., *Cheyenne Memories of the Custer Fight* (1995; Lincoln: University of Nebraska Press, 1998); Orin G. Libby, ed., *The Arikara Narrative of Custer's Campaign and the Battle of the Little Bighorn* (Norman: University of Oklahoma Press, 1998).

5. George P. Hammond and Agapito Rey, eds. and trans., *Don Juan de Oñate: Colonizer of New Mexico, 1595-1628*, 2 vols (Albuquerque: University of New Mexico Press, 1953), 1: 427.

6. Peter Nabokov, *Two Leggings: The Making of a Crow Warrior* (Lincoln: University of Nebraska Press, 1982).

7. Alfred A. Cave, *The Pequot War* (Amherst: University of Massachusetts Press, 1996), 133-134.

8. Inga Clendinnen, "Fierce and Unnatural Cruelty": Cortes and the Conquest of Mexico, *Representations* 33 (Winter 1991), 65-100.

BOOK COMMENTARIES II
The East and Pre-Nineteenth Century Wars

Sandy Antal, Canadian Forces Logistics officer (Ret.), and Ontario teacher; author of *A Wampum Denied: Procter's War of 1812* (American Library Association Choice Award winner).

Tecumseh and Procter: The Reason Why. The central theme of *A Wampum Denied: Procter's War of 1812* holds that the Anglo-Native alliance was more than a military pact of convenience, being driven by a political promise to the tribesmen that there would be no peace without the establishment of a homeland south of the Great Lakes. This commitment was clearly defined, officially endorsed, and actively pursued at the peace talks. Tecumseh's famous speech of September 18, 1813 (found in Richardson's *War of 1812* and elsewhere) first made me suspect that there was more to the allied connection than has been previously represented. He thundered out angrily, "When war was declared, our father told us he would get us our lands back which the Americans had taken from us."

My suspicions were confirmed with the discovery of a remarkable collection of documents held by the U.S. National Archives as "Miscellaneous Intercepted Correspondence, 1789-1815." Among these was a lengthy report written by the central figure in this struggle, Major-General Henry Procter. In it, he clearly articulated the allied aim of establishing a Native homeland "from the bottom of Lake Erie to the westward." His views further emerged in two obscure and anonymous writings, the *Quarterly Review* article "Campaigns in the Canadas" and the (very scarce) book *Lucubrations of Humphrey Ravelin*.

With this clearly defined war aim in mind, I turned to the Canadian National Archives to examine the writings of British authorities, only to find that the issue of a Native homeland was not only embraced by senior British commanders, but government officials as well. With the pieces of the puzzle assembled, I reconstructed the events from the stance of the commitment. Contrary to widely held opinion, Procter demonstrated considerable skill in marshaling slipshod resources to best three successive American offensives until overwhelmed by mass. Significantly, his offensive thrusts into Michigan, Ohio, and Indiana were as much preemptive as they were designed to honor the commitment to the Natives. Even on the disastrous Thames Campaign, Procter compromised his military judgment for reasons of "honor and policy," limiting his retreat to reassure the tribesmen that they would not be abandoned. At the disastrous battle of Moraviantown [or the Thames, 1813], Procter lost his reputation while Tecumseh lost his life and his people, their long cherished dream of a homeland. In his post-war writings Procter wrote, "They have been made the victims, not the pupils of civilization."

James Axtell, Kenan Professor of Humanities, College of William & Mary; author of *Natives and Newcomers* and *Beyond 1492*.

The book on Indian warfare that made the biggest impact on me when I was starting out in the late '60s was Douglas Leach's *Flintlock and Tomahawk*. Its depiction of warfare on both sides in King Philip's War was riveting, and its finding that the war was more damaging and lethal per capita than any other American war was stunning. Since then, I've profited from Patrick Malone's *The Skulking Way of War*, which treats in more detail warfare in New England from the Pequot War to King Philip's War [Metacom's War]. Jill Lepore's *The Name of War: King Philip's War and the Origins of American Identity* tells us less about the war itself than its reception and representation in American culture and historiography, but it's valuable for that reason. I'm also partial to *"Your Fyre Shall Burn No More,"* Joe [Jose Antonio] Brandao's iconoclastic and careful rewriting of the 17th-century wars of the Iroquois. He overturns a long historical tradition, beginning with Francis Parkman, that characterizes those wars as "Beaver Wars," conducted primarily by the Iroquois to seize beaver booty from enemy tribes. But Brandao proves conclusively that the

Iroquois raids were traditional sorties primarily for captives, honor, and revenge and not economic in origin.

Alfred A. Cave, professor of history, University of Toledo [Ohio]; author of *The Pequot War.*

I regard the most significant recent breakthrough in our understanding of the "Indian wars" to be the rediscovery of the crucial role of ideology in driving intercultural conflict and accommodation. My own work on the Pequot War has been grounded in the assumption that this episode cannot
be understood in purely materialist terms as the outgrowth of English land greed, but must be placed in a broader cultural context that gives appropriate weight to perceptions and misperceptions of the "Other." In seeking to understand shifting Indian responses to the Euro-American presence, I have been particularly influenced by writers who shed light on Native American revitalization movements. Anthony F.C. Wallace's invaluable essays on Indian revitalization movements and his superb study of Handsome Lake (*Death and Rebirth of the Seneca*) have been revelatory, even though Wallace does not deal directly with Indian wars.

Among more recent works, I have found David Edmunds's *The Shawnee Prophet,* Gregory Dowd's *A Spirited Resistance* and Joel Martin's *Sacred Revolt* particularly valuable. I regard our inability to reconstruct more of the Pequot understanding of the events leading to the 1837 massacre as a serious deficiency in our understanding of the Pequot War and in my own book on the subject. While the same problem impedes our study of other seventeenth century conflicts, the sources are richer and more revealing for later periods. The agenda, as I see it, must be to bridge the cultural gap that separates us from an understanding of the prophets and warriors who fought to keep the land free of Euro-American intruders. Skeptics are no doubt correct in their assumption that misunderstandings and misperceptions will persist despite our best efforts. But there can also be no doubt that such efforts will greatly enrich our understanding of Indian wars by moving us finally beyond both the "triumph of civilization" and the "Indian as victim" myths.

James David Drake, professor of history, Metropolitan State College of Denver; author of *King Philip's War: Civil War in New England*, 1675-1676.

Was King Philip's War [Metacom's War]—the decisive conflict among Indians and English in seventeenth-century New England—an unfortunate but inevitable byproduct of Euro-American progress, or was it a ruthless Puritan land grab? When I first approached the war, scholars had been polarized over this question for nearly twenty years. Douglas Leach's *Flintlock and Tomahawk* (1958), though unsurpassed as a thoroughly researched and richly detailed narrative, pitted "savage" Indians against "civilized" English. Seventeen years later, Francis Jennings' *Invasion of America* (1975) reversed this dichotomy by highlighting English "outrage bloody and barbarous."

Remarkably, I found that in both of these works the voices of the Indians—especially those who remained loyal to the English—seemed to get lost. The continuation of this near silence is even more startling considering the fact that Indian historians have made great strides in recovering the native past by combining the tools of traditional historians with those of anthropologists and archaeologists. Above all others, my model was Richard White's *The Middle Ground* (1991). Unlike any before, this book illustrates how Indians and European colonists, under the right circumstances, could find enough cultural overlap to accommodate one another for extended periods of time. White's work dealt with the Great Lakes region, but it prompted me to search for parallels in New England. Once I was able to weave a multiplicity of Indian perspectives into the narrative, Philip's War came to resemble a civil war—not just in its Indian versus Indian facet, but even English versus Indian.

The result of my research in *King Philip's War* has been controversial, but I hope productively so. My book avoids the style of many military histories that provide a virtual laundry list of battles, marches, and tactics; I couldn't improve upon Leach's ability to tell us who was where when. Instead, I pushed White's notion that Indians and English weren't inherently opponents to its logical limits by viewing Indians and English as members of a single society. King Philip's War, then, became a window on issues of identity, morality, and community. Hopefully this perspective provides a fruitful escape route from the tendentious arguments over Puritan morality that have dominated the literature—even if it's not as path breaking as *The Middle Ground*.

John K. Mahan, professor emeritus, University of Florida, and author of *The War of 1812* and *History of the Second Seminole War, 1835-1842*.

I became interested in Florida's Indian wars and got a start in writing on them while researching—mostly in the National Archives—my doctoral dissertation on the War of 1812, which eventually became a book. In it, I included some discussion of the First Seminole War (1816-1818), and this led me into research on the Second Seminole War (1835-1842). The University Press of Florida was interested in publishing the results but didn't have the funds. I took the unusual step of lending the press $2,500 to publish *History of the Second Seminole War*, and they paid me back from the profits on the sale of the book.

To readers interested in the Florida wars, I would recommend Frank Laumer's *Dade's Last Command* and Virginia B. Peters's *The Florida Wars*, the latter a decent work and the only one on all three Seminole wars. John T. Sprague's *The Origin, Progress and Conclusion of the Florida War,* first published in 1848, is a good source and was recently reprinted by the Seminole Wars Historic Foundation. One of the most interesting documents I've encountered is the diary of Lt. Henry Prince, which is now in the P. K. Yonge Library of Florida History at the University of Florida. It was published by the Seminole Wars Historic Foundation, with Frank Laumer doing the editing and with a foreword by myself.

As an aside, I wish to note that the wars of the eastern Indians have been neglected relative to attention paid to the horseback wars of the West. This results in a lopsided view of military relations between the white United States and the Native American.

J. R. Miller, professor of history, University of Saskatchewan; author of *Skyscrapers Hide the Heavens: A History of Indian-White Relations in Canada* [see "Book Notes" in this issue] and *Big Bear (Mistahimusqua).*

Robert S. Allen's *His Majesty's Indian Allies.* Canadian students of Native-newcomer relations for a long time found themselves both inspired and frustrated by the historiography on the diplomatic and military relations of Indians nations and Europeans during the period from the Seven Years' War (French and Indian War) to the War of 1812. Works by Jennings, Graymont, Calloway, and Edwards provided a wonderfully rich and persuasive account of the events on the North American continent that brought Europeans, colonists, and Aboriginal people together in alliance and conflict through this era. However, the focus of this historiography was fixedly on the region of present-day United States, and Canadians found their homeland and themselves relegated to the margins of the tale.

In 1992, Robert S. Allen's publication of *His Majesty's Indian Allies: British Indian Policy in The Defence of Canada, 1774-1815* (Toronto, Dundurn Press) shifted the focus on this familiar story north of the lower Great Lakes. Allen, a senior bureaucrat in the Department of Indian Affairs' Treaties and Historical Research office, re-examined the conflicts from a British and British North American point of view. The resulting account did not so much refute the work of earlier scholars as complement their findings. Allen put Canadians and First Nations that were based in or somehow related closely with Canadian territory back at the center of the struggle.

His Majesty's Indian Allies makes an important contribution, one that enriches the understanding of all students of these wars. Canadians can reread the story from a script in which their ancestors figure prominently, and non-Canadians interested in the topic can avail themselves of a more comprehensive depiction of the struggles by including Allen's work in their bibliography.

John Alden Reid, Park Ranger-Interpreter, Manassas National Battlefield Park (formerly Park Ranger-Historian, Horseshoe Bend National Military Park).

The Life of Andrew Jackson by John Reid and John Henry Eaton (Philadelphia: M. Carey, 1817). This narrative by a veteran of Andrew Jackson's campaigns in the Creek War in the wilderness of Alabama and in the War of 1812 is the first biography of the general who triumphed on the frontier against Red Sticks and Redcoats. It furnishes a glimpse into the camp of Jackson during the rigors and perils of the war. Captain, later Major, John Reid, Jackson's military secretary and aide-de-camp, was eyewitness to the carnage of the war, preparing Jackson's reports and correspondence, and recording impressions in diaries from which his narrative of Jackson's life is gleaned. Reid also describes the life of the Muskogee encountered during the wilderness campaigns from his observations, and his biography of Jackson thus constitutes a contemporary commentary of the Creek natives of Alabama.

Published posthumously in 1817, as Reid had died of typhoid pneumonia (or a mysterious fever) in 1816, his manuscript was completed by John Henry Eaton to benefit the major's orphaned children. The complete title of this earliest biography of General Jackson is *The Life of Andrew Jackson, Major General in the Service of the United States Comprising a History of the War in the South, from the Commencement of the Creek Campaign, to the Termination of Hostilities before New Orleans*. The biography was reprinted in a revised edition in Philadelphia by Samuel Bradford in 1824. Reid's original 1819 narrative was edited by Frank Lawrence Owsley, Jr., for publication by the University of Alabama in the 1970's. Unfortunately, the *Life of Andrew Jackson* by Reid and Eaton is now out of print, but can be found in libraries or through antiquarian booksellers. Perhaps, if curiosity regarding this earliest biography of Jackson is awakened anew, the book may be reprinted. Indeed, Reid offers a rare contemporaneous look at the Muskogee, their tactics in battle, and their military culture, while relating the vicissitudes Jackson and his militia suffered in the "pacification" of the Red Stick Creeks.

The biography focuses on Andrew Jackson's military experience, revealing the general's belief in discipline and his reliance on the bayonet in combat with natives. The *Life of Andrew Jackson* is an encomium to Jackson's military prowess. Reid is an obviously unabashed admirer of Jackson, rather refreshing to encounter today when revisionism has tarred the general with a brush of disdain. Reid's own words can elucidate the nature of his biography, and several quotations from the *Life of Andrew Jackson* will illustrate the themes discussed in this review.

As a staff officer, Reid was a witness to Jackson's personal bravery, as at the Battle of Enotochopco, where the militia was stampeded in panic by a fierce Red Stick attack: "In that moment of confusion, [Jackson] was the rallying point. . . . Cowards forgot their panic, and fronted danger, when they heard his voice, and beheld his manner. . . . In the midst of showers of balls, of which he seemed unmindful, he was seen performing the duties of subordinate officers, rallying the alarmed, halting them in their flight, forming his columns, and inspiriting them by his example."

Reid's own prose depicts the Red Sticks in combat, as at Tallusahatchee in November 1813: "Two [soldiers] were killed with arrows, which . . . . formed a principal part of the arms of the Indians; each one having a bow and quiver, which he used after the first fire of his gun, until an opportunity occurred for re-loading." At the Battle of Emuckfaw in January 1814, the Red Sticks fired from concealment behind fallen logs "prostrating themselves after firing." Also, the Red Stick practice of mutilating corpses is described, discovered at Emuckfaw: "our troops, who had previously fallen, had been raised, stripped, and scalped. Many of the Indians at Tohopeka were found in the clothes of those who had been killed and buried at Emuckfaw." The American slain at the Battle of the Horseshoe (or Tohopeka) were "sunk . . . in the [Tallapoosa] river, to prevent their being scalped by the savages," according to Reid. The origin of the "Red Stick" or "Red Club" name for the hostile Creeks is revealed by Reid: War clubs were used "on commencing hostilities; and which, when painted red, they consider a declaration of war." And again, "war clubs were immediately seen. . .particularly among the . . . hordes residing near the Alabama. Brandishing [red clubs] in their hands," the Red Sticks gathered for battle.

The character of Jackson's militia soldiery in the Emuckfaw-Enotochopco campaign is portrayed by Reid's observation, which speaks to the raw nature of the amateur army with romantic illusions: "Troops unacquainted with service are oftentimes more sanguine than veterans. The imagination too frequently portraying battles in the light of a frolic, keeps danger concealed, until suddenly springing into view, it seems . . . too hideous to be withstood."

These green troops embarked on a campaign to chastise the Red Sticks, but their departure was rather inauspicious, as Reid remarks: "Seldom . . . has there been an expedition undertaken fraught with greater peril than this. A thousand men, entirely unacquainted with the duties of the field, were to be marched into the heart of an enemy's country, without a single hope of escape, but from victory, and that victory not to be expected, but from the wisest precaution, and most determined bravery."

Reid also spoke of the audacious nature of Jackson in adversity. Reid eloquently evokes the brutal slaughter at the Battle of the Horseshoe: "Few [Red Sticks] escaped the carnage. Of the killed, many were thrown in the river, whilst the battle raged; many in endeavoring to pass it were sunk; and five hundred and fifty-seven were left dead on the ground. Among the number of the slain, were three of their prophets. Decorated in a manner wild and fantastic, the plumage of many birds about their heads and shoulders; with savage grimaces the corpses of the prophets were discovered on the field, one shot in the mouth by a grapeshot."

Major John Reid's *Life of Andrew Jackson* embodies a lucid eyewitness narrative of a combatant's experience and impressions of the cruel Indian war in the wilderness of Alabama in 1813 and 1814, where Jackson cut his first laurels of military fame. The brutality and sacrifice of the Creek War are compellingly related in Reid's biography of Jackson, which furnishes a contemporary and candid look at the frontier general whose fame eventuated in the presidency.

Donald B. Smith, professor of history, University of Calgary; author of numerous articles on Canada's native peoples and the early West of Canada.

What American historians have called the "Beaver Wars"—the struggles between the Hurons and their Algonquian allies against the Iroquois or Five Nations—have long fascinated historians. The Iroquois victory over the Hurons in l649-1650 remains one of the best known incidents in North American Indian history. Over the last twenty years new studies, rigorously researched and argued, have replaced older treatments. The works of Francis Parkman, great literary efforts that they may be, and George T. Hunt's *The Wars of the Iroquois* (1940) have little value by today's more demanding standards.

Basic historical texts on this important topic now include Bruce G. Trigger, *Natives and Newcomers: Canada's "Heroic Age" Reconsidered* (l985); Daniel K. Richter, *The Ordeal of the Longhouse: The Peoples of the Iroquois in the Era of European Colonization* (1992); Giles Havard, *La Grande Paix de Montréal de 1701: Les Voies de la Diplomatie Franco-Amerindienne* (1992); and Jose Antonio Brandao, *"Your Fyre Shall Burn No More": Iroquois Policy Towards*

New France and Its Native Allies to 1701 (1997). Trigger emphasizes cultural and economic causes for the conflict and ends his text in the mid-seventeenth century. Richter extends the discussion through the late seventeenth century to the early eighteenth. His captivating study, which like Trigger's, also stresses economic and cultural factors, relies largely on Dutch (in translation into English) and English documentation. It should be complemented by Havard's and Brandao's studies, which depend heavily on the French sources. Havard writes clearly and concisely. He introduces all the players in the struggle: the Iroquois, the Algonquinas (and their Huron allies), as well as the French and Dutch/English. Brandao's great strength lies in the number of French and Iroquois casualties he provides from very through research.

The year 2001 marks the 300th anniversary of the Peace Treaty made at Montreal in 1701, between the Algonquians, the surviving Hurons, the Iroquois and the French. Through these four modern studies, the interested reader can enter fully into the excitement of the "Beaver Wars."

Bruce Vandervort, Editor, *Journal of Military History*.

In the history writing business, older secondary sources tend to suffer from what E. P. Thompson once called "the enormous condescension of posterity." Taking seriously a nineteenth century history of an Indian war, for example, could just be enough to get your book dismissed out of hand by a lot of reviewers. As in so much else in our society, the newest interpretation of what happened and why in history is usually taken to be the best. I'm afraid I've been going pretty stubbornly against this modernist grain in the research I'm currently doing on the Creek War of 1813-14. H. S. Halbert & T. H. Ball's *The Creek War of 1813 and 1814*, originally published in 1895, not only has the advantage of immediacy (the authors, a pair of Baptist preachers, were able to interview people who had knowledge of the events of the Creek War) and a wealth of detail that is probably unavailable in any other source, but is as objective and balanced in its treatment as anything I have encountered from later periods. A marvelous antidote to both the Jackson fanatics and the apologists for the irresponsibility of Red Stick leaders!

John E. Worth, archaeologist, The Coosawattee Foundation; author of *The Timucuan Chiefdoms of Spanish Florida*.

The "Indian wars" and other frontier conflicts of Spanish Florida are not widely-known beyond scholarly circles, but nonetheless occupy an important place in the history of the early American colonial era. During Florida's "First Spanish Period" (1565-1763), there were numerous armed conflicts throughout the expanding Spanish frontier, though only a few were widespread enough to be of any import in historical records. Among the primary Indian provinces administered through the Franciscan mission system, there were several important rebellions, including the Guale rebellion in 1597, the Apalachee rebellion in 1647, and the Timucuan rebellion in 1656. This last major rebellion is examined in detail in my recent two-volume book , *The Timucuan Chiefdoms of Spanish Florida* (Gainesville: University Press of Florida, 1998).

What made the 1656 Timucuan rebellion different, and thus significant, was the fact that it represented a calculated attempt on the part of the Timucuan mission chiefs of northern Florida and southern Georgia to free themselves from the power of the military governor of St. Augustine, whose repressive policies undermined their chiefly authority, and whose tactless dealings with these hereditary nobles forced them to take up arms in defense of their birthright as Indian leaders.

In examining the roots of this conflict, and its aftermath and ultimate repercussions throughout Spanish Florida, I was led to delve deeply into the structure and function of the entire colonial system, revealing a downward spiral of epidemic disease, obligatory labor drafts, and eventual English-sponsored slave raiding. The 1656 rebellion was the starting point for a search that spanned more than a century of doomed Indian policy that witnessed the expansion and eventual collapse of a mission system comprising many tens of thousands of Southeastern Indians. Nevertheless, despite the eventual extinction of most of these groups and their near invisibility in the broader mentality of present-day America, their stories represent compelling portraits of the earliest colonial days in this country, and as such deserve a place among the broader literature about America's many Indian wars.

The Works of Rev. Francis Paul Prucha, S.J.

Patrick Jung

Every good student of the American Indian wars and United States Indian policy has heard the name of Rev. Francis Paul Prucha, S.J., a member of the Society of Jesus (or the Jesuits) who taught for many years at Marquette University in Milwaukee. Although he retired in 1990, he occasionally taught courses on United States Indian policy at Marquette for several years afterward. During the spring of 1991, I had the privilege of enrolling in one of his courses on United States Indian policy, and it started me on what has been a rich and fascinating scholarly interest in American Indians.

The instruction and mentorship that I received from Father Prucha have had a tremendous impact upon my research interests. Anyone familiar with his work knows that he has produced some of the most significant books on federal Indian policy, as well as the frontier army and the Indian wars. Exhaustively researched, based heavily upon primary sources, and dispassionately written, Prucha's books are indispensable resources for scholars and researchers.

Students of American Indian history would agree that Prucha's most significant work is *The Great Father* (1984). The culmination of more than thirty years of research on American Indians and their relationship with the United States government, *The Great Father* remains the seminal work available on this topic. Tracing federal and state policies toward American Indian tribes from the colonial era to the 1980s, *The Great Father* examines the Indian wars, missionary activities, "civilization" and education programs, and federal administration of Indian affairs. Virtually no aspect of the Americans

Indians' relationship with the United States and its citizens is overlooked. This makes *The Great Father* a valuable reference source, particularly for students of the Indian wars, because it provides excellent examinations of those aspects of federal policy and Indian-white relations that were directly and indirectly related to conflicts with the Indians, such as the trade and intercourse laws, the reservation system, government trade factories, Indian removal, the Dawes Act, and Indian boarding schools. Indeed, *The Great Father* is encyclopedic in its coverage.

Prucha's earlier works tend to be more narrow in their subject matter, but several are still of great interest to students of the Indian wars and the frontier army, particularly those who concern themselves with the region east of the Mississippi River. Prucha's first book was *Broadax and Bayonet* (1953), a published version of his doctoral dissertation that he completed under the famous Frederick Merk at Harvard University. Prucha's argument in *Broadax and Bayonet*, reminiscent of Frederick Jackson Turner's Frontier Thesis, is that the United States Army was the harbinger of American civilization on the frontier and was a crucial institution in the development of the Old Northwest from 1815 to 1860. *Broadax and Bayonet* was unique in its day because it was not traditional military history that examined battles and campaigns. It is really one of the first works of "New Military History" that looks at the social, economic, and cultural facets of the frontier army. It also established what would be the defining characteristics of Prucha's scholarship: meticulous and thorough research, expert use of federal records, and dispassionate, objective scholarship.

Prucha's next work, *American Indian Policy* (1962), examines the federal trade and intercourse acts that stood as the principal foundations of United States Indian policy between 1790 and 1834. In a very real sense, this book, his first on federal Indian policy, was the intellectual predecessor of *The Great Father*. The trade and intercourse laws, which regulated all contacts between whites and Indians, sought to control the fur trade, end the sale of illicit whiskey, stop intrusions onto Indian lands, and prevent and punish violence between the races. *American Indian Policy* deals primarily with the trans-Appalachian West during the early nineteenth century. Prucha wrote subsequent books on Indian policy and education that shifted the temporal focus to the late nineteenth century and the geographic concentration across the Mississippi. Two of the most notable in this regard are *American Indian Policy in Crisis* (1976), which examines Christian reformers and the Indians between 1865 and 1900, and *The Churches and the Indian Schools, 1888-1912* (1979).

Prucha has also produced several reference works that students of American Indian history and the frontier army will find useful. The first is *A Guide to the Military Posts of the United States, 1789-1895* (1964), which shows the location of every federal fort built in the continental United States and also provides a short history and bibliography for each installation. The *Guide to the Military Posts* also illustrates the numbers of troops at various points on America's frontiers between 1789 to 1895. Another valuable reference book is Prucha's *Atlas of American Indian Affairs* (1990), which provides maps for a wide variety of phenomena such as Indian land cessations, Indian removal, the locations of reservations, and Indian demography. The Atlas also reprints all of the maps that are found in Prucha's *Guide to the Military Posts*.

Prucha's most important contribution to the study of the Indian wars and frontier conflicts is *Sword of the Republic* (1969), which expands upon the thesis that he presented in *Broadax and Bayonet*. Prucha asserts in *Sword of the Republic* that the United States Army, in addition to serving as the harbinger of American civilization on the frontier, also served as an agent of American empire. Despite the fact that it was small, poorly financed and equipped, and hampered by a lack of support from Congress, the Army functioned to expand the United States geographically between 1783 and 1846 in wars against various Indian tribes and imperial rivals such as Great Britain and Spain. *Sword of the Republic* is a more traditional work of military history, and in it Prucha provides outstanding examinations of the Northwest Indian War, the First and Second Seminole Wars, the War of 1812, and the Black Hawk War. He also examines the army's role in policing the frontier, continental exploration, Indian removal, and other noncombat functions that were equally as essential to American expansion.

Prucha's most recent work is *American Indian Treaties* (1994), which considers the nature of treaty-making between the United States and the Indian tribes over the course of two centuries. Prucha labels Indian treaties a "political anomaly" that recognized Indian tribes as fully sovereign political entities while at the same time treating them as dependent wards. An earlier, related work by Prucha is *Indian Peace Medals in American History* (1971), which investigates the federal government's use of peace medals, usually embossed with the likeness of the president, as a means to insure strong, peaceful relationships with the Indian tribes. Certainly, tribal leaders desired these medals, many of which federal Indian agents and army officers bestowed upon chiefs after treaties of peace and friendship were negotiated.

The works discussed here do not include the numerous anthologies and collections of published documents edited by Francis Paul Prucha, nor have I included any of his articles, many of which are also very influential. Nevertheless, these are Prucha's most significant works, and all students of American Indian history should be aware of them. At some point in time, every serious scholar in this area will have the need to refer to at least one of these books. Given their broad coverage of both subject matter and primary sources, they are books that will stand the test of time and will shape our understanding of American Indian history for generations to come.

Works Cited

American Indian Policy in Crisis: Christian Reformers and the Indian, 1865-1900 (Norman: University of Oklahoma Press, 1976).

American Indian Policy in the Formative Years: The Indian Trade and Intercourse Acts, 1790-1834 (Cambridge: Harvard University Press, 1962).

American Indian Treaties: The History of a Political Anomaly (Berkeley: University of California Press, 1994.)

Atlas of American Indian Affairs (Lincoln: University of Nebraska Press, 1990).

The Churches and the Indian Schools, 1888-1912 (Lincoln: University of Nebraska Press, 1979).

Broadax and Bayonet: The Role of the United States Army in the Development of the Northwest, 1815-1860 (Madison: State Historical Society of Wisconsin, 1953).

The Great Father: The United States Government and the American Indians, 2 vols. (Lincoln: University of Nebraska Press, 1984).

A Guide to the Military Posts of the United States, 1789-1895 (Madison: State Historical Society of Wisconsin, 1964).

Indian Peace Medals in American History (Madison: State Historical Society of Wisconsin, 1971).

The Sword of the Republic: The United States Army on the Frontier, 1783-1846 (New York: Macmillan Company, 1969).

BOOK COMMENTARIES III
Camp, Custer, and the Little Bighorn

Aaron L. Cohen, owner of Guidon Books (Guidon Books, 7117 West Main Street, Scottsdale, AZ 85251).

The book that sparked my interest in the Indian wars and started me on a journey that eventually led to the opening of Guidon Books was *The Custer Myth*, by Col. William A. Graham. I purchased the book when it was first published in 1953. Not only was the mystery of what happened at Little Bighorn intriguing, but the book also contained a great bibliography complied by Fred Dustin. This, of course, gave me a list of books to start collecting. I could not resist the challenge.

I was living in Southern California at the time, and there were several great booksellers in the area, including Arthur H. Clark, Dawson's, Maxwell Hunley, and International Bookfinders. With these resources at my disposal, I figured my chances of finding the books I wanted were greatly improved. So, my Indian wars and Custer book collecting days began. My wife, Ruth K. Cohen, who was already a fine Civil War historian, also became interested in the Indian wars. For many years our summer vacations alternated between visiting Indian war battlefields and Civil War battlefields. During this time we amassed quite a collection of books.

In 1963, we decided to turn our avocation into a business and open a bookstore devoted to the Civil War and Western Americana. After much debate, we picked up stakes and relocated to Scottsdale, Arizona, where we started Guidon Books. When we opened for business, we were greeted by a welcoming committee of local merchants to whom we explained the concept of our specialty book store. As they were leaving, we overheard one of them say to the others, "They won't last six months!" He was wrong, of course, and on August 1, 2000, Guidon Books commenced its thirty-seventh year at the same location on Main Street in Scottsdale. At last count we had over 500 titles devoted to the Indian wars, both on the Plains and in the Southwest. Overall, we carry about 1,500 books covering various topics related to the American Indians Culture.

I have most enjoyed reading such authors as Col. Graham, Edgar Stewart, Dan Thrapp, Stephen Ambrose, Paul Wellman, Robert Utley, and of course, Frederic F. Van De Water. There are also a host of relatively new authors, including Jerome Greene, Richard Allen Fox, Jr., and Jeffrey Wert, who bear watching. With the advent of the Internet, historians and writers are able to conduct research that they would not have been able to do in the past without expending a great deal of travel. As a consequence, we are seeing new books published on the Civil War, the Indian wars, and the American West that may not have been feasible before. Thankfully, interest in these themes is still high, and the number of new topics, newly discovered source material and perspectives is far from exhausted. Someday, I suspect I will see a book titled *The Custer Myth —Solved!*

David C. Evans, author of *Custer's Last Fight.*

During my early years of research I was greatly influenced by three books. These were *The Custer Myth*, by W. A. Graham, *Custer's Luck*, by Edgar I. Stewart, and *Legend Into History*, by Charles Kuhlman. Graham impressed me by providing source material so the reader could form his own opinion. Stewart impressed me with the objectivity of his analysis, a trait sadly lacking by many who have written about the battle. Kuhlman impressed me with his research methodology. Being an engineer by profession, I'm driven to seek detailed answers and understand the interrelationships of events. This battle and the associated personalities represent a very complex subject requiring a thorough and lengthy examination. Graham's work influenced me to provide the source date contained in the eighteen appendices of my book *Custer's Last Fight*, and Stewart's work influenced me to make sure I presented both sides of the controversies, not just my conclusions.

Richard G. Hardorff, editor of *On the Little Bighorn with Walter Camp*, and author of *Cheyenne Memories of the Custer Fight.*

I have several favorite authors on the subject of Custer, the Battle of the Washita, and the Battle of the Little Bighorn. These include Walter M. Camp, for his untiring efforts to obtain information from participants of the Plains Indian wars; Edgar I. Stewart, who wrote *Custer's Luck*, which is a classic of disciplined writing; Dr. Richard A. Fox, for his talents to combine history with his field of archeology in *Archaeology, History, and Custer's Last Battle*, and the publications of James Willert, for his research talents to compile detailed, factual information on the Indian Wars.

Paul L. Hedren, superintendent, Niobara National Scenic River; author of *Fort Laramie in 1876* and *Traveler's Guide to the Great Sioux War.*

To single out a favorite Indian wars book is a challenge. I've been a reader of Indian wars history for some four decades, and recall in my most impressionable years pouring again and again through Edgar Stewart's *Custer's Luck*. In a great and grand way, his mastery of detail and clear prose cemented my fascination with the monumental Indian campaign of 1876, and I still think it ranks among the top five or ten books on the Little Bighorn. I also think very highly of Bob Utley's *The Lance and the Shield*. In his uniquely intuitive and insightful way, Bob obliges us to view the Great Sioux War through Indian eyes. Other modern-day scholars are pushing this perspective too, but none have yet demonstrated Utley's mastery. I must say that I am also very deeply taken by Larry Sklenar's *To Hell With Honor*. In this day when everyone's writing a Custer book and so many are of such dubious quality, newcomer Sklenar has crafted a provocative look at Custer and the Little Big Horn that has the hallmarks of a classic. I don't throw about such kudos frequently, but I truly like this book and believe it will have staying power.

So what is my favorite Indian wars book? Today, my vote goes to Don Rickey, Jr.'s *Forty Miles a Day on Beans and Hay: The Enlisted Soldier Fighting the Indian Wars*, a gem from 1963 and still in print. This one, too, I devoured again and again in my formative years. While one could still do so, in the 1950s Rickey communicated personally with dozens and dozens of Indian wars veterans and with some engaged in thoughtful, long exchanges. In many ways, Rickey authenticated our visions of the frontier regulars first fashioned in Charlie King's novels and later made all the more colorful, if stereotypical, in John Ford's epic cavalry movies. *Forty Miles a Day on Beans and Hay* presents unvarnished truths about soldiering during a compelling era in American history, showing that these men were neither saints nor sinners, Indian haters nor lovers, but mere commoners faithful to an oath and unrelenting duty. This work led me to years of living history gamesmanship with the National Park Service and General Miles Marching and Chowder Society, driven as I was to experience as best as I could some of the same rigors of frontier soldiering. It provokes me still in an array of continuing scholarship on these common, and yet uncommon, men of the Indian wars.

James Hutchins, Smithsonian Institute, author of *Boots and Saddles at the Little Bighorn* and editor of *The Papers of Edward S. Curtis Relating to Custer's Last Battle.*

When asked to say how long I've been hooked on Custer and the battle of the Little Bighorn, I almost said forever and ever. In honesty, I have to admit that only some sixty years have gone by since I got that way. The condition set in, I'm quite sure, in 1936 when I sat spellbound through several showings of a Cecil B. De Mille thriller entitled *7th Plainsman*, with its glimpses of Custer. That moved me to explore the local library's holdings regarding the general, consisting of two books with starkly differing images—Frederick Van de Water's *Glory Hunter* and Frederick Whittaker's *A Complete Life of Gen. George A. Custer.*

A little later, I wrote to the Anheuser-Busch folks in St. Louis, saying that, if there might be an extra copy of their famous lithograph, "Custer's Last Fight," lying about the brewery, there was a kid in Columbus, Ohio, who sure could use it. And behold! A few days later arrived a mailing tube holding that wondrous image with all its glorious, gory details. It formed the chief decoration in my bedroom for years. I was most decidedly hooked.

As evidence that the condition persists, not long ago I was privileged to edit a remarkable body of papers, soon to appear in print, containing the findings of the celebrated Indian photographer and ethnologist Edward S. Curtis when he inquired into the Little Bighorn engagement nearly a century ago. Typically, Curtis made his investigation on the very spot, interviewing three Crow Indians who had served Custer as scouts and who claimed to have stayed with him up to the very beginning of the fight. Fascinating stuff, whatever one's conclusions regarding the scouts' story.

Although the days when it was possible to meet face to face with Indians who had been present beside the Little Bighorn at the time of the celebrated battle are long since gone, they existed even into my own time. I remember well standing beside Tongue River one sweltering summer day in 1953, listening as a venerable Cheyenne Indian recall the time when, as a boy of about ten years, he stood beside his mother atop the benchland west of the Little Bighorn and gazed toward the heights across the river. He remembered the racket of gunfire and the pall of smoke and dust enveloping the struggle that white men would come to call "Custer's last fight." An unforgettable moment indeed!

Douglas C. Keller, ranger-interpreter, Pea Ridge National Military Park (formerly interpreter at Little Bighorn Battlefield National Monument).

I can't say I have a favorite Indian wars book. There are so many available one must be discerning and choose wisely. I would like to recommend some of the more noteworthy titles that have helped shape my knowledge, particularly relating to Little Bighorn. The first is *Custer's Luck*, by Edgar Stewart. This is a rare example of a book that has withstood the test of time. Despite the fact it was written in the 1950s, it remains one of the more objective, well-researched books on the campaign. It's only weakness is that archeological research has brought great changes to how we interpret the demise of Custer's battalion.

I am partial to personal accounts. For this reason I am very fond of Walter Camp's notes in *Custer in '76*. Sgt. Charles Windolph's diary, *I fought with Custer*, is another excellent work. Dr. Thomas Marquis's *Wooden Leg* is one of the better firsthand studies of Plains Indian culture and events of 1876 from the Cheyenne viewpoint. A weakness of the book is that Marquis blended the stories of several warrior veterans including Wooden Leg, into one person's experiences. For this reason, the chapter on Little Bighorn needs to be read with a grain of salt. Wooden Leg is in too many places for just one person. Finally, all of the publications covering the archaeological work at the battlefield are of great value. Archaeology has brought us a more clear understanding of how Custer's command met its fate.

The only thing harder than recommending the best books on Little Bighorn would be to name the worst. There are too many of them! Pushing aside all the dime novels, I would have to nominate Mari Sandoz's *Battle of the Little Bighorn* as the all-time worst. The book is riddled with factual errors and apocryphal statements. There is not a single note on any page, and the book is so biased that it reveals more about the writer than about the battle. My crowning reason for not liking the book is that it is so widely read among the general population. Sandoz remains a popular writer, and as such, her books significantly shape the views of her readers. There is very little a park ranger can do in a twenty minute talk to correct the myths and misconceptions generated by pop literature. But rest assured, we will keep trying!

Neil Mangum, superintendent, Custer Battlefield National Monument; American Battlefield Preservation Project historian.

In my long-standing association with Little Bighorn Battlefield National Monument, I am frequently asked my favorite works on the battle. Unequivocally, I place Edgar Stewart's *Custer's Luck* on my short list. This book has literally withstood the test of time. Originally published in 1955, it is still in print. Its longevity is remarkable considering that a new publication on the Custer fight seemingly emerges on a monthly basis, most of which quickly pass into obscurity because they leave little impact or they offer nothing new or substantive on the topic. *Custer's Luck* has been read by more students of the battle, serious and casual, than any other book with the possible exception of the battlefield's handbook.

There are innumerable reasons for the continued success of *Custer's Luck*. First, it is comprehensive. Stewart adroitly infuses critical context so that the reader is indoctrinated with the sequential events leading up to the Seventh Cavalry's departure from the Yellowstone River. No books before, and few after, have accomplished this in Stewart's scope and detail. Second, Stewart has no axe to grind. He does not play partisan favorites in the story log. He simply lays out the information and allows the readers to draw their own conclusions. In the chapters surrounding the battle of the Little Bighorn where personalities dominate pages and absorb the most ink, his abstention from attacking or defending characters is all the more remarkable. That is not to say that Stewart dodges controversies: he does not. Rather, he confronts them head on by presenting all viewpoints to an issue, then summarizing his findings based on his analysis. Virtually nothing slips by Stewart, whether it is analyzing Terry's orders to Custer, the debate over Thompson or Davis creek route, or the size of the Indian encampment. While footnotes are a bane and a turnoff to many readers, I enjoy them. Stewart's more so, because within the footnotes is a story line that supports his textual narrative and conclusions.

Stewart's interpretation of Custer's last hours is somewhat outdated considering that new data in the form of letters, diaries, interviews, and several archaeological surveys has provided contemporary scholars grist upon which to reinterpret the battle. Despite new interpretations, I am reminded of Stewart's wisdom on treatment of the last stand: "[T]here are almost as many theories about the battle as there are people to have theories. And as a general rule one is as good as another, for, while we may lack sufficient evidence to prove that such and such a thing happened, we also lack, except in a few cases, enough evidence to prove that something else did not happen. If we cannot prove one theory, neither can we disprove another."

Stewart, a Michigander, studied history at Harvard and the Universities of Washington and California. He was a long-time Distinguished Professor of History Emeritus at Eastern Washington State University. Dr. Stewart died on November 24, 1971. In 1946 Stewart served as a seasonal interpreter at what was then called Custer Battlefield National Monument. The story goes that park superintendent Edward Luce was displeased with Stewart. It seems that Stewart spent too much time conducting research for his book and neglecting the needs of the park visitors. The next summer, Luce did not invite Stewart back to the battlefield as historical aide. True or not, we can be thankful that Stewart accomplished his research even if it came at the expense of the visitors. In the long run, we have all benefited from reading *Custer's Luck*, a classic by all standards in the field of Little Bighorn scholarship.

Ron Nichols, California, author of *In Custer's Shadow: Major Marcus Reno*, and editor of *The Reno Court of Inquiry*.

Having been involved with this particular period of Western Americana for more than thirty years, my focus, from the very start, has been on the Little Bighorn battle. Why this particular event? This battle was not especially significant in the course of developing the western frontier, but it had that one element which continuously appeals to me: mystery. I want to know what really happened on that hot Sunday afternoon in June 1876.

The only book, in my opinion, that provides sufficient information to determine, at least to some degree, of what occurred at the Little Bighorn is *The Reno Court of Inquiry* published by the Custer Battlefield Historical & Museum Association in 1993. This is the only official testimony of most of the surviving Seventh Cavalry officers present at the battle. I have found myself referring back to this book so often that I have literally worn out one copy—the pages are now falling out of the book.

When asked about the "best books on the battle," there are two other books I recommend: Edgar I. Stewart's *Custer's Luck*, and John Gray's *The Centennial Campaign*. Although neither is without error, both provide a good understanding of the events leading up to the battle and the battle itself. What is the best book on the 1865-1890 Indian Wars? It is most definitely Robert Utley's *Frontier Regulars*.

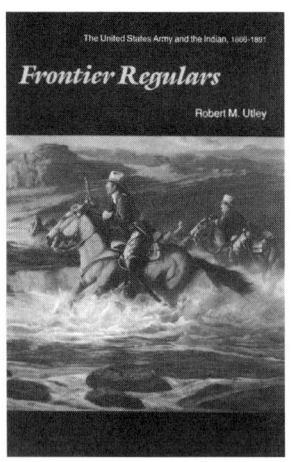

Interest in the Little Bighorn continues to produce new books every year, some good and some a rehash of old material. Will a book come along that resolves the mystery of the Little Bighorn? Probably not to anyone's complete satisfaction. The controversy about almost every aspect of the battle and its participants will continue to generate new interest and new theories for years to come.

Brian C. Pohanka, Virginia, consultant for The History Channel and Time-Life Books; co-editor of *Miles Keogh* and *Nelson A. Miles: A Documentary Bibliography of His Military Career*.

Rummaging through my overflowing library shelves as I attempted to answer the daunting question, "what is your favorite Indian Wars book?" and realizing there were a number of volumes that might qualify for that distinction, I found myself thinking, "Well, if I had to pick my favorite Indian wars researcher, that would be easy—Walter Mason Camp."

I have been fascinated with the battle of Little Bighorn since childhood, drawn like so many others to the controversies, theories, personalities and mysteries of "Custer's Last Stand." And that interest has never waned, because there is always something "new" to be discovered, some fresh approach or reevaluation to apply. But I had never heard of Walter Camp until 1976, when I encountered the Brigham Young University Press publication, edited by Kenneth Hammer: *Custer in '76: Walter Camp's Notes on the Custer Fight.*

Nothing in Walter Camp's background presaged his eventual interest and formidable contributions to the history of Little Bighorn and the Indian Wars. Born in 1867, the Pennsylvania native spent his entire professional career as a highly regarded civil engineer, employed by various railroad companies. A longtime editor for the *Railway and Engineering Review*, his only published work was a two-volume technical treatise, *Notes on Track*. But, like many amateur historians then as now, Walter Camp became fascinated with "Custer's Last Stand," and for some thirty years devoted as much time as he could to researching the Battle of the Little Bighorn.

What made Camp unusual, and his work of particular value, was his effort to seek out and interview veterans of that fight—Army officers, enlisted personnel, civilian and Indian scouts, and the warriors who had vanquished Custer's Seventh U.S. Cavalry. Camp made a number of extended visits to the battlefield, tracing Custer's approach with men who had taken part in the 1876 campaign, and used his surveying talents to prepare detailed maps of the terrain. In time Camp's interests broadened to include other Indian wars campaigns, all the while recording, in his characteristic scrawl on various scraps of paper, the words of those who had *been there*.

The fact that Camp was open-minded and eminently reasoned in his approach to Little Bighorn makes it all the more unfortunate that he did not live to write a history of Custer's last campaign. Following his death in 1925, Camp's papers were dispersed, and his contributions unrecognized—until Kenneth Hammer's publication of *Custer in '76*. It was the most exciting book on the battle I had ever read, as so much of it was fresh, vital primary material. Other Camp notes have surfaced in the 24 years since Hammer's

ground-breaking compilation, and found their way into print: *Camp on Custer: Transcribing the Custer Myth*, edited by Bruce R. Liddic and Paul Harbaugh, was published by The Arthur H. Clark Company in 1995, and *Camp, Custer, and The Little Bighorn*, edited by Richard G. Hardorff, was published by Upton & Sons in 1997. All are well worth reading, pondering, and learning from, and are a lasting tribute to a remarkable researcher, Walter Mason Camp.

(For additional information on Walter Camp, see the article by Sandy Barnard in this issue.)

Larry Sklenar, U.S. Department of Defense, retired; author of *West-Fever* and *To Hell With Honor: Custer and the Little Bighorn* (see book review in this issue)

No one has done more to advance our understanding of the Indian wars than Walter Mason Camp. The shame is that he died before he could pull together the raw materials amassed over more than twenty years of amateur investigation, chiefly with respect to the conflict of white and Indian cultures on the Great Plains of the American West.

While collecting material for my book *To Hell With Honor: Custer and the Little Bighorn* (University of Oklahoma Press, 2000), I was of course aware of Camp's work, chiefly through published compilations of selected letters and interviews by Kenneth Hammer and others. But when I purchased microfilm copies of a significant body of Camp material from the Harold B. Lee Library at Brigham Young University, I realized what a truly extraordinary job the railroad man had done and what a great service he had performed—and all in his spare time. The bits and pieces I gathered from the Camp collections housed in the Denver Public Library and the Lilly Library at Indiana University increased my admiration for the man.

Walter Mason Camp did not realize his own dream of writing a definitive account of the disaster that befell Lt. Col. George Armstrong Custer and the Seventh U.S. Cavalry at the Battle of the Little Bighorn. More's the pity.

However, one suspects from reading the record that whatever his urge to organize and write that account, he could not stop accumulating information, always in search of that final letter or interview that would fix the event in his mind. His death at fifty-eight years of age ended whatever hope he still harbored of authoring that book, but given the choice of more time, he surely would have preferred to seek out and interview one last survivor, leaving others to gather whatever glory is derived from saying what was said to him.

No one has done total justice to the work of Walter Mason Camp. Bless the likes of Kenneth Hammer. Bless the institutions that care for the collections he left behind. But in this age when oral histories of any noteworthy event are the rage, it is fair to say that Camp was very much ahead of his time and that he deserves the attention accorded many lesser lights.

I have it in my mind that it would be a wondrous thing if some brave soul could undertake to make a true compendium of the railroad man's amateur inquiries into Indian war history. It won't be me, and more's the pity.

Richard Upton, founder of Upton & Sons, Publishers; author of *The Custer Adventure* and *Fort Custer on the Big Horn* (Upton and Sons, Publishers, 917 Hillcrest Street, El Segundo, CA 90245).

The Four Most Important People in my "Custer Adventure." I had no way of knowing, when I first met Frankie Maynard in 1956, that it would be the beginning of a relationship that would result in our marriage in 1958. The next year, 1959, we traveled to Billings, Montana, to visit Frankie's family. There I was introduced to Brevet Brigadier General George A. Custer and the Battle of the Little Bighorn.

During this time, we visited the family farm homesteaded by my wife's grandfather, Henry Carl Klenck, who served in the First U.S. Cavalry at Fort Custer, Montana Territory, from May 1887 to March 1892. The farm, located along the Yellowstone River in an area called Lockwood Flats, turned out to be a gold mine of early Montana history. Henry Klenck has remained at Fort Custer in a civilian capacity until it was abandoned in 1898, and he kept photographic albums of pictures of his contemporaries at the fort. Almost all of the photos were taken by O. S. Goff. Family members eventually made all of Klenck's material available to me, including a field officer's desk, copies of the *Winners of the West* newspaper, Custer Battlefield artifacts, letters, branding irons, and even flags that had flown over Fort Custer. Klenck died in 1935 after becoming a leader in the Indian wars veterans organizations, and was the subject of many *Billings Gazette* feature articles.

When I traveled to the Custer Battlefield National Monument, as Little Bighorn Battlefield National Monument was then called, I purchased my first books on the battle—*Custer's Luck*, by Edgar Stewart and *The Custer Myth*, by Col. W. A. Graham—which I immediately read. Noting that Col. Graham's wife, Helen Bury Graham, was mentioned in the acknowledgments, and that she was a neighbor of mine in California, I resolved to call her upon my return home. Mrs. Graham was receptive to my call and even invited Frankie and me to her home, a practice that occurred at least once a year for many years. Of course, our conversation was mostly about her late husband's Custer interest. I learned that Col. Graham had been a close friend of Gen. Douglas MacArthur, and I was naturally curious to know whether Graham had broached the subject of Custer with MacArthur; he had not. Mrs. Graham did put me in contact with another close friend of Col. Graham's whom, she said, had all of her husband's papers, letters, and books. She told me that this friend, Hugh Shick, was the most knowledgeable person she knew on the subject of Custer. When I contacted him, I found that he indeed was everything she claimed!

So began a relationship with Hugh and Penny Shick that lasted until their deaths. During the years of my interest in Custer, I have met [and published] most of the top scholars on the subject. If they knew Hugh Shick at all, they would in no way take offense when I said that Hugh Shick was the "Babe Ruth" of Custer scholars. He never wrote any books, but if you look at the acknowledgements of almost every Custer book of the period you will find his name mentioned. He was simply the best.

So thank you Frankie Maynard, Henry Carl Klench, Helen Bury Graham, and Hugh Shick for the added dimension you have given to my life and the lives of all of us who are fascinated by the history of the American West.

Robert M. Utley, [U.S.] National Park Service, retired; author of *Cavalier in Buckskin* and *Frontier Regular*s.

Likes and Dislikes. I should begin with the Battle of the Little Bighorn because there's where I began when Errol Flynn launched me toward George Armstrong Custer in 1942. I still regard John Gray's two books [*The Centennial Campaign* and *Custer's Last Campaign*] as by all odds the most perceptive and incisive. In more recent years I have gained high respect for Greg Michno, who has brought a healthy skepticism to prevailing interpretations and pieced together alternatives that make sense. Richard Hardorff has made some original contributions. Finally, Larry Sklenar, in the recent *To Hell with Honor*, brings to the subject a lifetime of analyzing intelligence for the government and produced some fresh and provocative interpretations.

On the negative side, probably a measure of royalty envy, I judge *Son of the Morning Star* a stream-of-consciousness abomination. That may be unfair because I never got beyond the first twenty pages. [Author Evan S.] Connell made the millions I thought belonged to me. But that's the fickle reading public.

On the larger stage, some very good work has been done by Jerome Greene, Paul Hedren, and Michael Tate. In the Southwest, let's celebrate the many excellent volumes of Dan Thrapp while paying tribute to the two biographies of Ed Sweeney [*Cochise* and *Mangas Colorado*].

Regrettably, most of the popular volumes of the past, from Paul Wellman to Ralph Andrist, are distinguished principally by superficiality. And a caution to all readers: waste no time on anything either Mari Sandoz or Stanley Vestal wrote under the guise of history.

Let's face it, in this day of the *Dances with Wolves* syndrome, our field is not crowded with people who want to study war. If it were, someone would long since have superseded my military volumes, which, incidentally, had the misfortune to appear during the *Little Big Man* years of Vietnam.

WALTER MASON CAMP
My Favorite Researcher of the Little Bighorn

Sandy Barnard

When Lt. Col. George Armstrong Custer and his Seventh U.S. Cavalry clashed with a coalition of Plains Indian Tribes along the Little Bighorn River in southeastern Montana, the battle took no more than a few hours on a hot afternoon nearly 125 years ago. Yet ever since, the participants' actions of June 25-26, 1876, have been endlessly analyzed.

Scores of historical sleuths have sought to unravel the mysteries of the celebrated fight, but it remains as unfathomable today as the day Custer challenged his Indian foes. Yet countless individuals have focused their research on the 1876 battle. The early generation included William Graham, Charles Kuhlman, E. A. Brininstool, Edgar Stewart, and J. W. Vaughn. Prominent writers across the decades have included Don Rickey, Kenneth Hammer, John Gray, John M. Carroll, Lawrence Frost, and Robert M. Utley. Today's crowded field of astute battle observers include Jerry Greene, Jim Willert, Richard Hardorff, Gregory Michno, and Richard Fox. However, my own choice as my favorite Little Bighorn researcher of the last 125 years may be surprising—Walter Mason Camp. Camp never wrote a book about the battle and is vulnerable to criticism on that very point. As Don Rickey once said, "Camp didn't do enough writing. All he did was collect facts."[1]

Maybe so, but others view Camp's collection of "facts" as the most important source of data about the battle. Historical consultant Brian Pohanka says, "Camp was far and away the single most important historian of the Little Bighorn—a very great man to whom all of us owe a great debt."[2] As Hammer and Dennis Rowley wrote, "Armed with a tireless pen, an intense burning interest in the western Indian wars, an indefatigable will, and not least, a railroad pass, he quietly and doggedly established a legacy for himself and those he interviewed that will live forever in the annals of American Indian history."[3]

Custer in '76: Walter Camp's Notes on the Custer Fight, Hammer's classic study of Camp's research, gave Hammer's subject legendary standing among the Little Bighorn fraternity.[4] Camp, described as "a quiet, unassuming man," is an odd person to historical accolades. By training a civil engineer and a railroad man, he spent his working years as a journalist editing a railroad magazine. For more than twenty-five years he spent his spare time to researching the Little Bighorn and other Plains Indian battles.[5] He proved all too human in one important, and regrettable, way: one more fact always beckoned, and his quest continued, delaying forever the writing of his own battle interpretation.

Camp was born April 21, 1867, at Camptown, Pennsylvania, to Treat Bosworth Camp and Hannah A. Brown. As a youth, he worked on farms and in the forests. By age sixteen, he was a track walker for the Lehigh Valley Railroad, his first job in what stretched into a forty-two-year career in railroading. In 1891, he completed his studies in civil engineering at Pennsylvania State College. In the years that followed, he held a variety of posts: surveyor in Fresno, Calif.; draftsman in San Francisco for the Southern Pacific Railway; construction engineer, then superintendent of operations for the Rainier Avenue Electric Railway in Seattle; and various positions for the Seattle Lake Shore and Eastern Railway. In 1895, Camp was a graduate student in electrical and steam engineering at the University of Wisconsin at Madison, and in 1896, taught in the National School of Electricity in Chicago.

Finally, in 1897, Camp began a twenty-five-year career in Chicago as engineering editor of the *Railway and Engineering Review* (later *Railway Review*). Reportedly, Camp never failed to deliver his weekly column.[6] As Rowley and Broadhurst pointed out, "As a writer Walter Camp commanded the respect of the railroad fraternity. He had a thorough knowledge of the practical side of railroading, and knew railroad conditions and needs."[7]

More important for history, Camp focused his avocational energies on the Indian Wars and especially the Battle of Little Bighorn. Possessing a journalistic style as meticulous as any modern reporter's, Camp did what few other researchers could do: he investigated the Little Bighorn wherever facts could be found. In his greatest contribution, while traveling for his railroad

Walter Mason Camp, circa 1920, in a photo probably taken on his farm in Lakeville, Indiana. *John Husk Collection*

magazine or on vacation, he tracked down the living sources—probably 200 survivors of various western battles, both white and Indian—and he recorded their stories for future generations.[8] Initially, Camp focused on Custer's last fight, but eventually he broadened his research to include such engagements as the 1868 Battle of the Washita, Ranald Mackenzie's 1876 raid on Dull Knife's village in Wyoming, Frank Baldwin's 1876 fight with Sitting Bull on Redwater Creek in Montana, the Nez Perce Campaign of 1877, and the death of Sitting Bull and the clash at Wounded Knee in 1890. He visited some 40 battlefields, and he supplemented his many field interviews by correspondence with dozens of battle veterans. "He was a trailblazer in his zeal to record the facts of history from the people who had witnessed that history," Hammer has noted.[9]

His correspondence with numerous people, notably Mrs. Elizabeth B. Custer, Brig. Gen. E. S. Godfrey and First Sgt. John Ryan, makes clear that he was a "Custer man." For example, in a May 1920 response to Godfrey, Camp apologetically tells the retired general, "You think my remarks unfair to General Custer where I say, in connection with the fighting of August, 1873, that 'on both of these occasions Custer was looking for trouble,' etc. I have written . . . to eliminate those words and all that follow them in that paragraph, as I know that your judgment is superior to mine in such matters, and I do not want to do any injustice to General Custer or his memory."[10]

In July of 1920, he told Mrs. Custer: "I think I have had a pretty good outline of the gossip and scandal that were current in the 7th Cavalry in the days of the Pioneer West, but that is not history. As for General Custer, I have often remarked that I considered him one of the most useful officers who campaigned against Indians, and that impression is what really counts in the historical sense. What history wants to know is the service which men performed, and this opinion of mine has been well supported by my interviews with such men as General Godfrey, Colonel [Charles] Varnum and General [W. S.]Edgerly."[11] Camp's last comment to her on this subject may be most revealing: "What I have heard about the affairs of the 7th Cavalry that I do not intend to write about for publication would make a big book."

What ignited Camp's interest in the Little Bighorn is unclear, but that letter to Mrs. Custer provides a glimpse into his motivation: "This battlefield site is the shrine of all the West. The fact that the Indian life of the Plains has passed, or is passing, away makes it all the more so. This landmark belongs to the heroic. Here the Indian power of the Plains attained its utmost strength, and here it won its last victory. From that moment it began to decline, and in the short space of but a few years it had dwindled to a state of helplessness. The supreme sacrifice of General Custer and his brave men was made at this turning point."

Camp probably began searching as early as 1903 for battle survivors, Indian and soldier, to interview along the back paths of America's West, and he continued until about 1920. However, his busiest period fell between 1908 and 1914. His supplementary letter writing also continued throughout his active research. Initially, Camp envisioned writing a narrowly focused book to be titled "History of the 7th U. S. Cavalry." In 1908, in writing to First Sergeant Ryan, a Little Bighorn survivor, Camp summed up his purpose: "For five years I have been engaged at leisure times gathering matter for a history of the Little Bighorn campaign. I have the co-operation of more than 30 surviving officers and enlisted men of the 7th Cavalry. . . . I have been on the Custer battlefield and on both of the Reno battlefields several times, and have surveyed and mapped them. . . . I have interviewed Indians on the reservations who fought against Custer and against you fellows on the hill." Camp added: "In this book the enlisted men will receive attention as well as the officers, and I am therefore calling upon all hands to assist me with information in order that the history may be as accurate as possible."[12]

Hammer and Rowley described Camp's three-part methods as "simple but effective."[13] The procedure was to:

> 1. Find the desired person. Hammer and Rowley note that Camp was unceasing in his efforts. For example, on one occasion he hired a horse and wagon for a trek of many miles to interview one Indian at Interior, South Dakota.
> 2. Ask questions. Camp told Mrs. Custer that he spent eight hours discussing with General Edgerly the movement that Company D under Capt. Thomas Weir and then-Lieutenant Edgerly made to today's Weir Point.[14] Camp also relied on questionnaires to gather information by mail. One he sent to Ryan in 1908 consisted of nine tightly structured questions keyed to specific battle events that Ryan would know about.
> 3. Record answers. The results of Camp's research may be found today in major collections at Brigham Young University, Indiana University, the Denver Public Library, the University of Colorado at Boulder and Little Bighorn Battlefield National Monument.[15] Scraps of paper, envelopes, even matchbooks—all served to record his scribblings about a battle or a participant. Hammer and Rowley state, "He wrote in pencil and remarkably, the notes are still legible. He wrote clearly and firmly in a very readable style." Other researchers may think less of Camp's handwriting.[16]

Camp felt compelled to walk where his subjects had fought, and he became renowned for his expertise on many fields of combat. Through his efforts a marker was installed in the Wolf Mountains where Custer's command crossed the divide to follow Reno Creek to the Little Bighorn. As he told Mrs. Custer, "One cannot form an adequate idea of just what the situation was that confronted Gen. Custer that Saturday night and Sunday morning without being on the ground."[17]

Unfortunately, Camp's gathering of facts ended all too early. Only 58 years old, he died Aug. 3, 1925, at Kankakee, Ill. A series of letters he wrote in his last years to researcher George Bird Grinnell not only suggest why Camp never finished his book but also reveal his deep frustration at his inability to complete his long-cherished task.[18] In 1912, Camp and his wife, Emeline, bought a dairy farm in northwest Indiana, fifty-five miles from their Chicago home, intending it as a retirement place. By the early 1920s, an economic downturn forced Camp to handle much of the farm's chores himself. "In consequence," he told Grinnell in October 1923, "I had to get a leave of absence from my editorial job and come down here and attend to the farm myself. . . ." The Camps wanted out of the dairy business, he said, but economic conditions were against them. "So I am stuck as a farmer until we can sell out." He added, "I am all but out of the journalistic job, as I am now writing only weekly editorials. If I can sell the farm I shall quit journalism altogether and look for something that has less routine."

The letter to Grinnell reveals his longing to head west again, a point that became even more clear thirteen months later in a November 1924 letter: "Am now making improvements (to the farm) and hope to be able to sell it before another year. If I can do that I will be in good shape to go to work again on my western studies. I have in mind to take an auto truck + go west for a trip of six months or longer just as soon as I can get free from this farm work, which I care nothing about."

His deep frustration is equally evident: "As long as I was with the *Review* I could get no time for historical writing, by reason of so much traveling. So I have never done anything toward putting my Army book in shape for publication." Sadly, he died only nine months after reporting his hopes of proceeding to writing. A flyer promoting the sale of Camp's book collection suggested he may have been farther along on his book than his 1924 letter indicated. "At the time of his death, he had, ready for the press, a biography of General Custer, describing in detail his expeditions against the Indians, which would have been accorded a place among the foremost Americana items. He had, however, forgone its publication at the request of Mrs. Custer. who desired that it not be published until after her death." Other than an introduction, no manuscript has ever been found.[19]

After his death, other battle researchers eagerly sought Camp's notes. Six weeks after Camp died, Grinnell wrote his widow a letter that underscored the importance of her husband's research: "I feel that it would be a public misfortune if all the work that he did in gathering this material should be lost. The matter ought to be saved, and Mr. Camp ought to receive the credit for the great amount of time, labor and money that he expended in bringing it together." He concluded that "in the death of your husband America has suffered a real loss."[20]

Others anxious about his collection soon appeared. In May 1926, George B. Utley of Chicago's Newberry Library asked Mrs. Camp to consider donating or selling the material to his facility. He wrote, "Much, if not all (of the collection), would be highly desirable for our Indian collection."[21] A year later,

Lt. Col. C. A. Bach of the Army War College's Historical Section made a similar request, while offering his belief that "the information he gathered concerning Indian operations and activities had real historical value."[22]

Despite such appeals, Mrs. Camp retained her husband's vast collection, even after setting a price of $5,000 for it.[23] Eventually, through the dogged efforts of such men as Robert S. Ellison, who was an avid collector of Western Americana, Brig. Gen. William Carey Brown, and Grinnell, Camp's papers were preserved. In 1933, at the height of the Depression, Emeline Camp sold—for only $500—a large portion of her husband's papers to Ellison through Brown, who acted as his agent. While Brown had the papers, he apparently determined that portion weighed 50 pounds.[24] While $500 was a considerable sum for that period, today Camp's papers would demand top dollar from modern collectors.

Unfortunately for modern scholars, Camp's collection is scattered about the country in public and private hands. How that came to be is itself an interesting sidebar to his Little Bighorn research. By 1937, Brown had transferred the papers to Ellison.[25] Other researchers, including author Charles Kuhlman, also had access to the notes. After Ellison's death in 1947, some of his Camp holdings were donated to the Lilly Library at Indiana University. In 1967, after Mrs. Ellison's death, more items went to the collection at Lilly. Beginning in 1968, another large segment of Camp papers was acquired by the Harold B. Lee Library at Brigham Young University (BYU), and a smaller segment went to the Denver Public Library. Hammer edited the materials at BYU for publication in his 1976 book *Custer in '76*.

Yet another set of Camp notes surfaced in the mid-1980s as an indirect result of the battlefield's archaeological projects. After Camp's death, the Kenneth Roberts family moved in with Mrs. Camp to help her care for her invalid sister. In a closet sat five boxes of papers, including photographs, which the sister gave to the Roberts after Mrs. Camp's death. Naomi Roberts, whose married name was Dettmar, retained the boxes. By coincidence, she settled in Manitou Springs, Col., where in 1944, Ellison was mayor. "People tried to buy parts of her collection over the years, but she wouldn't sell them piecemeal," said John Husk of Denver, who participated in the archaeological projects. After Mrs. Dettmar saw Husk featured in news accounts of the battlefield digs, she contacted him.[26] Through his efforts, she donated her Camp materials in 1986 to the National Park Service archives at present-day Little Bighorn Battlefield National Monument.

The major segments of Camp's papers, including those at BYU, Indiana University, and Little Bighorn Battlefield, are now indexed and attract scholars and casual researchers alike. Hammer and Rowley summed up the importance of Camp's collections in this way: "Amidst the controversy that has swirled around the memory of Custer and his 'last stand,' embroiling literally hundreds of writers and collectors, Camp's notes appear as a welcome beacon. Among the dozens of interviews, all of them valuable and irreplaceable, are many that will be of more than passing interest to scholars and collectors."[27]

Camp's work offers small facts that enlighten almost every aspect of the Little Bighorn battle or its personalities. For example, in 1908, John Ryan revealed to Camp that he had written a 650-page manuscript about his Civil War and Seventh Cavalry experiences.[28] In June 2000 that manuscript, long believed lost, was sold to this writer by its owner. Often, a major issue is addressed in the Camp materials. Rumors suggested that Custer committed suicide, but Ryan, who directed the detail that buried Custer, told Camp that he had closely viewed the body: "In regard to the rumor that Custer shot himself, I do not think he ever did such a thing, nor do I believe that anybody knows who shot him."[29]

Camp's field notes are the single most important body of research materials for anyone seeking to learn more about Custer's battle with the Sioux and Cheyenne or other Indian fights. As Hammer and Rowley stated: "Camp's notes do not begin to allay all of the many controversies surrounding Custer and the Little Bighorn. In general . . . they help to lay to rest most of the questions about who was where. The significance of Camp's work will no doubt grow."[30]

NOTES

1. Conversation with author, Aug. 5,1994, Billings, Mont.

2. "An Interview with Brian C. Pohanka," [Little Big Horn Associates] *Newsletter*, March, 1995, 4-5.

3. Hammer, Kenneth, and Dennis Rowley, "Custer's Man Camp, Oral Historian Without Peer," *Manuscripts*, vol. XXVII, No. 2 (Tyler, Texas, Spring 1975),112-120.

4. See Hammer, Kenneth, ed., *Custer in '76: Walter Camp's Notes on the Custer Fight* (Provo, UT: Brigham Young University Press, 1976).

5. Rowley, Dennis, and Neil Broadhurst, "A Register of the Walter Mason Camp Papers," Mss. 57 (Provo, Utah: Archives and Manuscripts, Special Collections, H. B. Lee Library, Brigham Young University, 1981), 2.

6. Hammer and Rowley, "Custer's Man Camp," 114.

7. Rowley, Broadhurst, A Register, 5.

8. He reportedly had a limited ability to speak Lakota "Sioux" and other Indian languages. Brown, William C., "Records of Indian War History," undated newspaper clipping, Camp Collection, Little Bighorn Battlefield National Monument, Crow Agency, MT.

9. Hammer, *Custer*, 2.

10. Camp to W. S. Godfrey, May 19,1920, Elizabeth Bacon Custer Collection, Little Bighorn Battlefield National Monument (hereafter LBBNM).

11. Camp to Elizabeth B. Custer, July 15,1920, Elizabeth Bacon Custer Collection, LBBNM.

12. Camp to John Ryan, Nov. 19,1908. Camp Collection, Lee Library, Brigham Young University.

13. Hammer and Rowley, "Custer's Man Camp," 115.

14. Camp to Elizabeth B. Custer, Oct. 4,1920, Elizabeth Bacon Custer Collection, LBBNM.

15. Smaller quantities of Camp-related documents, principally correspondence, may be found in other public or private collections.

16. Hammer and Rowley, "Custer's Man Camp," 115.

17. Camp to Elizabeth B. Custer, Aug. 19,1919, Camp Collection, LBBNM.

18. George Bird Grinnell Collection Southwest Museum Library, Los Angeles.

19. "The Private Library of Walter M. Camp," flyer, Camp Collection, LBBNM.

20. George Bird Grinnell to Mrs. Walter M. Camp, Set. 15, 1925, letter in the possession of John Husk.

21. Utley to Mrs. Camp, May 29, 1926, Camp Collection, LBBNM.

22. Bach to Mrs. Camp, Jan. 21, 1927, Camp Collection, LBBNM.

23. Athor's interview with Ken Hammer, Nov. 19, 1994.

24. Brown, William C., "The W. M. Camp Records of Indian War History," undated record, Ken Hammer Collection, Box 4, LBBNM; Letter to Mrs. Camp, June 27,1933, Camp Collection, LBBNM.

25. Letter from Bruce R. Liddic to author, Dec. 29, 1994. Liddic edited private Camp materials for publication in 1995. In this collection, Liddic reviewed numerous letters by Mrs. Camp, Brown, Ellison, and others that may shed additional light on efforts to pry loose the notes from the widow. However, the owner of this material has not made it available to other researchers. Liddic told the author that a 1937 letter from Brown to Ellison made clear that all the material had been transferred to Ellison by that time.

26. Telephone interview with John Husk, March 31, 1993.

27. Hammer and Rowley, "Custer's Man Camp," 117.

28. Ryan to Camp, Nov. 29, 1908. Segments dealing with seven of his ten years with the Seventh Cavalry were published in 1908-09 in his hometown newspapers in Newton, Mass. Camp Collection, Lee Library, Brigham Young University.

29. Ryan to Camp, Dec. 17,1908. In 1885, Ryan interviewed Sitting Bull, when Buffalo Bill's Wild West Show played in Boston. Ryan's description of the one wound going through Custer's body from right to left is inaccurate . Most experts believe Custer was shot on his left side. Camp Collection, Lee Library, Brigham Young University.

30. Hammer and Rowley, "Custer's Man Camp," 120.

Ten Essential Books

Understanding the Battle of the Little Bighorn

Compiled by Michael A. Hughes

Over a year ago, I began asking students of the Battle of the Little Bighorn to single out the books they found utterly essential for understanding the events that led to and took place at that famous engagement of June 25-26, 1876. Compiling a select reading list would presumably be difficult and the results controversial. The fight had, after all, inspired more books and articles than had all other clashes of North America's Indian wars combined. In addition, as James Willert's article (above) indicates, the interpretations of various researchers have varied greatly.

Surprisingly, the informal survey found almost complete consensus upon the value of the work of three particular authors: Edgar I. Stewart and the more recent scholars John S. Gray and Robert M. Utley. The publications of five other authors were also repeatedly recommended. The list of the "ten essential books" below represents the works most frequently and enthusiastically endorsed by serious readers, interpreters, and authors. The compilation is based on the comments and suggestions of over thirty-five persons, most of whom are identified in the thanks below. (I apologize to any individuals whose names have been inadvertently omitted, and to those authorities who were not contacted during this rather unsystematic query.)

THE LIST

1. Fox, Richard, *Archaeology, History and Custer's Last Battle* (Norman: University of Oklahoma Press, 1993)—While some readers found Douglas D. Scott, et al.'s interpretations of "Custer's last stand" in *Archeological Perspectives on the Battle of the Little Bighorn* (Norman: University of Oklahoma Press, 1989) more credible, there is agreement that Fox had produced a thought-provoking reexamination of Custer's possible movements from the most current forensic evidence.

2. Gray, John S., *The Centennial Campaign: The Sioux War of 1876*- (1976; reprint, Norman University of Oklahoma Press, 1988)—This book was almost universally cited as the finest single campaign overview. Nearly all later authors have drawn on Gray's work.

3. ———, *Custer's Last Campaign: Mitch Boyer and the Little Bighorn Reconstructed* (Lincoln: University of Nebraska Press, 1991)—Gray's time and motion analysis in this biography of Custer's mixed-race scout was considered invaluable by many who commented.

4. Hardorff, Richard, editor, *Camp, Custer, and the Little Bighorn: A Collection of Walter Mason Camp's Research Papers on General George A. Custer's Last Fight* (El Segundo, CA: Upton and Sons, Publishers, 1997)—Walter Mason Camp's papers were considered essential primary research material. Kenneth Hammer's *Custer in '76: Walter Camp's Notes on the Custer Fight* (Norman: University of Oklahoma Press, 1990) and Bruce R. Liddic and Paul Harbaugh's *Custer and Company: Walter Camp's Notes on the Custer Fight* (Lincoln: University of Nebraska Press, 1995) were also well recommended. However, Hardorff in particular earned praise for his editorial insights and his annotations.

5. ———, editor, *Cheyenne Recollections of the Custer Fight* (1993; reprint, Lincoln: University of Nebraska Press, 1997)—*Lakota Recollections of the*

Custer Fight (Lincoln: University of Nebraska Press, 1999) also received endorsement but the collection of Cheyenne primary material seemed to be regarded as the more badly needed of the two compilations of Indian accounts.

6. Michno, Gregory F., *Lakota Noon: The Indian Narrative of Custer's Defeat*, by Gregory F. Michno (Missoula, MT: Mountain Press Publishing Company, 1997)—This book is the closest yet to a convincing time and motion account for the Indian side and may be the most success in weaving together and reconciling Indian oral histories. As with Sklenar's book below, no one agreed with every one of Michno's conclusions, but all still felt that this was a unique work that had to be taken seriously.

7. Sklenar, Larry, *To Hell with Honor: Custer and the Little Bighorn* (Norman: University of Oklahoma Press, 2000)—No one who commented totally agreed with Sklenar's bold, fresh reinterpretation of the battle, but all felt that the book had inspired worthwhile debate and deserved respect for its scholarship and intelligence. Remarkably, the work seems to be approaching "classic" status less than a year after publication.

8. Stewart, Edgar I., *Custer's Luck* (University of Oklahoma Press, 1955)—Despite the lack of access to archaeological evidence and oral history that has become available since its publication, readers felt that this lengthy book is an unusually durable source of reliable information. Everyone queried who has done interpretation at Little Bighorn Battlefield recommends Stewart.

9. Utley, Robert M., *Cavalier in Buckskin* (Norman: University of Oklahoma Press, 1991)—Utley's perceptive biography of Custer, while concise, was recommended as unusually readable, well rounded, and authentic.

10. ——, *The Lance and the Shield: The Life and Times of Sitting Bull* (New York: Henry Holt, 1993)—Utley's biography of the charismatic shaman Sitting Bull was judged one of the best researched and most perceptive on a major Indian figure at Little Bighorn. Though Sitting Bull may

not have played a direct part in the battle, this book on his life was regarded as worthwhile to gaining an understanding of the background of the event.

When comments were expanded to cover works on the entire Great Sioux War of 1876-1877 and not just the Battle of the Little Bighorn, several additional books were also frequently recommended. The result is a select reading list on the entire war elsewhere in this issue.

Our thanks to Sandy Barnard, Aaron Cohen, Jim Court, David C. Evans, Jerome Greene, Barry Hagan, Richard Hardorff, Paul Hedren, Paul Hutton, Jerry Keenan, Douglas Keller, Michael Koury, Louis Kraft, John D. McDermott, Neil Mangum, Greg Michno, Jim Mundie, Ron Nichols, C. Lee Noyes, Brian Pohanka, Glenn Robertson, Jerry L. Russell, Larry Sklenar, T. A. Swinford, Rodney Thomas, Richard Upton, Robert M. Utley, and to several anonymous members of the staffs of Fort Larned National Historic Site, Fort Laramie Historical Association, Fort Laramie National Historic Site, Little Bighorn Battlefield National Monument, North Dakota Historical Society, Southwest Parks and Monuments Association, U.S. Army Combat Studies Institute, and Washita Battlefield National Historic Site.

BOOK COMMENTARIES IV
The Rest of the West

Paul Beck, professor of history at Wisconsin Lutheran College.

There have been a number of excellent books published in the last few decades dealing with the Indian wars. Most of them I have found interesting and enjoyable, but the book that I consider one of the best general works on the Indian Wars comes from the 1960s, Ralph K. Andrist's *The Long Death: The Last Days of the Plains Indians*, published in 1964. Along with Dee Brown, author of the better known *Bury My Heart at Wounded Knee*, Andrist was one of the first historians who tried to humanize Native Americans and approach the Indian wars with some objectivity. *The Long Death* deals with the wars against the Plains Indians from the American Civil War (1861-1865) to Wounded Knee (1890). Andrist was sympathetic to the Native Americans without turning them into saints, and was critical of the white civilians, army, and federal government officials who opposed them, but without becoming shrill or biased. Today, it is quite common for historians to point out the prejudice, mistakes, and naked aggression of the white Americans of the time but in the early 1960s, when TV westerns that depicted Indians as savage and bloodthirsty still reigned, Andrist's work was ground breaking.

What also makes *The Long Death* an appealing book is its comprehensiveness. Andrist not only covers the major wars with the Dakotas, Cheyennes, and Comanches, but also the smaller wars against the Bannock, Sheepeaters, and Utes. Andrist also gives attention to the Dakota War of 1862 in Minnesota and the Sand Creek Massacre in Colorado, viewing them as the natural starting points for the latter wars on the plains. His writing style is clear and engaging.

I first encountered *The Long Death* as a young farm boy in rural Minnesota. Now, many years later, as a professor doing my own research and writing on the Indian wars, I still find myself thumbing through Andrist's book and using it as a source. I consider it a fine example of good research and history.

Pete Brown, founder and owner of History America Tours (History America Tours, P.O. Box 797687, Dallas, TX 75379).

As a purveyor of expeditions relating to great events in American history, my favorite Indian wars book is closely tied to one of my favorite Indian wars sites. Fort Bowie National Historic Site in southeastern Arizona features the melted adobe ruins of the fort and a magnificent 2.4 kilometer hiking trail from the parking lot to the ruins.

In order for one to fully comprehend all that happened along that historic trail and at Fort Bowie, Robert M. Utley authored *A Clash of Cultures: Fort Bowie and the Chiricahua Apaches*, a 1997 publication of the National Park Service.

In just 88 pages, Utley presents the story of the Chiricahua Apaches and their ongoing struggles with the Spanish, Mexican, and American "intruders." The text and illustrations, along with the maps and suggested readings, give the reader a precise overview of a most significant phase of the Indian wars.

One learns initially about the various Apache groups and the Chiricahua homeland in the mountains and valleys of Apacheria. The nomadic life in a "harsh land" is described with an emphasis on the importance of warfare and the esteem in which successful warriors were held. The patterns of raid and retaliation that held true during the nineteenth century conflicts with the Mexicans and Americans are graphically portrayed.

The importance of the location of the Apache Springs and the route of the Butterfield Trail sets the sight for the 1861 "Bascom Affair" and the resultant "Cochise Wars" (1861-1863) [of the Apache Wars, 1861-1886]. All of this becomes very real as one traverses the trail in the shadows of the battle of Apache Springs. Geronimo's dealings with Crook and Miles are woven into the narrative, as is the final surrender. The memorable picture of him and Naiche standing together at Fort Bowie awaiting their departure to Florida provides a fitting close. This small publication by Utley is essential to any Indian wars library and retains a prominent place in mine.

James V. Court, former superintendent of Little Bighorn Battlefield National Park; owner of Custer Tours (Action Travel and Custer Tours, P.O. Box 310, Hardin, Montana 59034).

While not technically Indian wars books, all of the writings by James Willard Schultz give an insight into the life and times of the Plains Indians (primarily Piegan Blackfeet), which is helpful in understanding their relationship to the invaders and their attachment to their families and the land. Only a couple of his titles are still in print: *Blackfeet and Buffalo* and *My Life as An Indian*. Many others, however, are available in libraries.

Publisher Mike Koury suggested I read the Flashman books (a fiction series), and I eventually got around to reading *Flashman and the Redskins*. The book is amusing (sexy) and—at least the Custer parts—pretty well presented historically. It was nice to get a good survivor story. I recommend it.

Jerome A. Greene, research historian, [U.S.] National Park Service; author of *Lakota and Cheyenne Indian Views of the Great Sioux War, 1876-1877* and *Nez Perce Summer, 1877*.

While there are several works by Robert M. Utley that I greatly admire, my overall favorite Indian wars book remains his *Last Days of the Sioux Nation* (New Haven, CT: Yale University Press, 1963). This study explores the events that culminated in 1890 in the massacre of Lakota Sioux Indians along Wounded Knee Creek, South Dakota, together with the incidents of the tragedy itself and collateral actions in the immediate vicinity into early 1891. I believe this work should be a mandatory read and a continuing reference for any person with a serious interest in Indian wars history and particularly in the broader aspects affecting the Lakotas' experience in their relations with whites.

For this exercise, however, I am more interested in promoting the volume as a learning tool for historians and writers. Not only is the book (in my opinion) the finest ever produced about this most critical episode in U.S.-Lakota relations as well as in Lakota tribal history, but it provides one of the clearest examples available of what good history is all about. It shows what can result from solid research coupled with synthetic yet appropriately detailed narrative and a fluid writing style, topped off by objective analysis.

This is not to say that there have been no changes in the field of history (or in the Wounded Knee story, for that matter) over the thirty-eight years since its publication; notably, modern data-collecting methods are far more sophisticated and comprehensive, and today's historians have available to them a more complete record in the published literature of the years leading up to Wounded Knee; there is also today easier accessibility to sources, including to new ones that have appeared since 1963. Too, there have been changes in terminology. (The present inclination to use the term "massacre" versus the earlier "battle" in referencing the event, for example, stems partly from this book.)

Nonetheless, *Last Days of the Sioux Nation*, which is still in print, offers students the complete illustration of well executed Indian wars research and writing, and could serve as a graduate school model on how best to practice the historian's craft. Further, writers without formal history training who are interested in researching and writing about the Indian wars might consider this book as an example of how to establish historical context, to say nothing of the proper use of evidence and of accuracy of presentation. And for those readers who might be interested in ever so briefly stepping beyond Custer, I most heartily recommend this early work by America's premier frontier military historian.

Michael A. Hughes, [Oklahoma] East Central University; managing editor, *Journal of the Indian Wars*.

If asked to identify the first book relative to the Indian wars that had an impact on me, I would have to say Alvin M. Josephy's *The Patriot Chiefs* (1961; reprinted 1994). The book is a classic work of historical writing and seems as readable and informative today as it was forty years ago. I remember how startling the book's title was when I saw it on a library shelf as a child. Josephy challenged over three centuries of American assumptions about the morality of westward settlement and forced assimilation. He presented Indian leaders not as the ignorant enemies of Americanism and progress, but as freedom fighters defending legitimate nations from destruction. It was the kind of book that could shift the mental ground beneath a young reader's feet.

My ancestors had not had the distinction of either actively battling the United States or enduring the catastrophe of removal to Indian Territory. They had instead been part of the forgotten "remnant" population of Indians quietly and systematically dispossessed through the scheming of southeastern state officials. My forbearers were not spoken of proudly—being neither glorious white conquerors nor noble victims, they were seldom spoken of at all. Josephy's book eventually made me proud of my ancestors by teaching me not just that there was a right to resist "manifest destiny" but that resistance took many forms. He increased my admiration for our Tecumsehs and our Cochises. But he also helped me see that any Indians who managed to simply survive through decades of incessant persecution and deprivation were heroes as well.

John C. Jackson, independent scholar; author of *Children of the Fur Trade* and *The Piikani Blackfeet*.

The call for commentaries on favorite books on the Indian wars recalls that flowering of interest in military history that followed the Second World War and Korea. As veterans completed their studies under the GI bill and wrote their books, those who had known a great global conflict celebrated predecessors who participated in the conquest (or loss) of North America. One obscure but essential study of the neglected contests in the Pacific Northwest is *Frontier Steel* by Waldo E. Rosebush (Spokane: Eastern Washington State Historical Society, 1958).

While most literature of the Indian wars focuses on the dramatic encounters on the Great Plains, *Frontier Steel* follows the First United States Dragoons in the years between the Mexican War (1846-1848) and American Civil War (1861-1865). Spread thin, the dragoon companies operated from the Apache country of the southwest to the plateau country of eastern Washington. To even the often nearly overwhelming odds they faced, the soldiers relied on their recently issued Colt-Walker dragoon revolvers. *Frontier Steel* contained illustrations of two revolvers that were recovered from a battlefield, weapons whose condition spoke of a defeat. During the desperate retreat of the ill-fated 1858 Steptoe expedition, the Spokane and their allies closed in on the fleeing column near Spokane Lake in Washington Territory. One pistol found on the battlefield was frozen because of a broken spring. Even more telling, the other was found fully operative with two charges still unfired in the cylinder, rusty testimony to the fate of the man who held it. After being plowed out of the wheat fields that currently occupy the battleground, the guns were placed in the collection of the Eastern Washington Historical Society. Despite the setback of Edward Steptoe's defeat, the "little wars of destiny " in eastern Washington decided the fate of the Yakima, Walla Walla and Spokane nations and were a forecast of the later engagements fought on the Great Plains. Waldo Rosebush filled his book with a wealth of data, maps, lists of engagements and rosters of officers that make it an invaluable compendium on a neglected part of western history.

Jerry Keenan, retired publisher; author of *Encyclopedia of the American Indian Wars* and the newly revised and expanded *The Wagon Box Fight* (2000).

Choosing one's favorite book on the Indian wars is not just a challenge—it presents a bona fide dilemma, because so many possibilities immediately come to mind. If the assignment asked instead for my favorite book on a specific war or battle, the challenge would be a little less daunting. But only a little less. Be that as it may, my choice is Robert Utley's *Frontiersmen In Blue* (1967) and *Frontier Regulars* (1973). For the purpose of this exercise I have taken the liberty of viewing these two volumes as a single entity.

I offer three reasons in support of my choice. First, the coverage is comprehensive. Anything of significance relating to the Indian wars of the West between 1848 and 1890 may be found between the covers of these volumes. Second, they are solidly researched and do an outstanding job of synthesizing a vast body of information to present a well-organized and lucid picture of the Western Indian wars. I should point out, too, that these books, like Utley's other works, help the reader see and understand the events of which he writes in the larger context of history. Finally, the author's fluid narrative style of writing makes these siblings an enjoyable reading experience as well.

Over the years since they first joined my library, *Frontiersmen In Blue* and *Frontier Regulars* are numbered among the most used volumes on my shelves. For anyone interested in building an Indian wars library, I cannot imagine a better place to begin than with these two works of Robert Utley.

Gregory Michno, independent historian; author of *Lakota Noon* and *The Mystery of E Troop*.

When I was a student in high school in the mid-1960s, I began to write down the title of every book I read, a practice which I have kept up. As I look back on the lists, I can see that I have averaged about one book a week for thirty-five years. A lot of darn books. And a great number of them were about the American West and the Indian wars.

To choose the best book on the Indian wars, or a favorite, is a daunting task. I will avoid that by naming a few of those I found most influential. Now, "influential" is a relative word. They may not all have been the most scholarly, accurate, watersheds, or earth-shakers, but for me, starting out into the wide-world of books, young, somewhat idealistic and romantic, they were seminal.

Paul Wellman's *Death on the Prairie* (1934) and *Death in the Desert* (1935) were probably the first general surveys of Indian conflicts in the West that I read. A smooth-flowing narrative adventure was perfect at the time. George Bird Grinnell's *The Fighting Cheyennes* (1915) served the purpose of providing the Indian point of view. Something similar was found in George Hyde's *Red Cloud's Folk* (1937). More blood and thunder, with a good balance of emphasis between sides, was discovered in W. S. Nye's *Carbine and Lance* (1937). While Nye concentrated on Fort Sill and the southern plains conflicts, Remi Nadeau covered the north, in *Ft. Laramie and the Sioux* (1967), Of course, there is also Robert Utley's *Frontiersmen in Blue* (1967), and *Frontier Regulars* (1973), a two-volume survey of western Indian wars that is an even-tempered and objective accounting of over 40 years of strife.

However, truthfully, the most influential writer for me has to be Mari Sandoz. Although her scholarship has been disparaged of late, she certainly was a fine writer. For a boy delving into the world of western adventure, she was the catalyst to get the dream juices flowing. Books such as *Crazy Horse* (1942), *The Buffalo Hunters* (1954), *The Cattlemen* (1958), *Love Song to the Plains* (1961), and *The Battle of the Little Bighorn* (1966) were my favorites for many years (even though Custer was *not* seeking to become president, as Sandoz claimed in the last book.)

In closing, I must add one recent book that I thoroughly enjoyed: Ronald Becher's, *Massacre Along the Medicine Road* (1999). This book contains everything (and more) that you thought you could learn about the Indian War of 1864 within Nebraska.

John C. Monnett, professor of history, metropolitan State College of Denver; author of *The Battle of Beecher Island and the Indian War of 1867-1869* and *Tell Them We Are Going Home: The Odyssey of the Northern Cheyennes.*

As an impressionable undergraduate deciding whether to major in history or biology, the book that undoubtedly drove me over the edge, (to history of course), was Paul I. Wellman's *The Indian Wars of the West* (1947). First published in two volumes as *Death on the Prairie* (1934) and *Death in the Desert* (1935), my 1960s combined edition introduced me to a side of the Indian wars I had never considered. During my extended childhood, I thrilled to a host of Hollywood westerns at the Saturday matinee where the good guys were always white and the heroine was always rescued from "evil savages" led either by Geronimo or Sitting Bull—or so it seemed. Paul Wellman's work was my wake-up call. Here were not only Geronimo, Sitting Bull, Custer, and the Seventh Cavalry as I had never before considered them, but such little known yet exciting events as the fight at Turley's Mill in New Mexico in 1847, and an Apache raid on Nacori, Sonora, on April 10, 1930.

Not only did the author's prose enrapture me, Wellman also set me on my current course to developing an expanded world view of the Indian wars, one I must confess came as quite a shock to a naive mid-western suburbanite in 1964. At first I wondered why anyone would want to include the Indian side of the story. More than a few scholarly articles and professional conference presentations have identified Dee Brown's *Bury My Heart at Wounded Knee* (1970) as the single most important book to influence the current wave of "New Western History." By presenting, supposedly for the first time, the Native American view of the Indian wars to a wide audience, Brown has been credited with pointing out cultural diversity in the West, despite the critics' denunciations of his book as less than superlative history. Was Brown unaware of Wellman or did he simply ignore him? Wellman's work is not listed in Brown's bibliography, despite both authors being published by Doubleday. But Brown did dramatically steal Wellman's thunder according to current perceptions. My forty-year-old copy of Wellman is rich with balanced history and cultural convergence. So, this type of broad vision has actually been around since the 1930s. Wellman first made me aware that the story of the Indian wars as a national story rather than a one-sided, nationalistic chronicle. His book has influenced my writing viewpoint more than any single volume. Despite its now faded and tattered brown dust jacket, it still occupies an honored place on a bookshelf in my study.

During the last thirty-six years I have served as a tour guide at museums and historic sites that deal with the history of the Indian wars in the Great Plains region of the U.S., literally hundreds of visitors who have had their interest "tweaked" during the tour have asked me to provide them with the title of a good reference book that would give them a good "general" background of the whole era. The answer, of course, is that there is no ONE reference. It depends upon the particular interest level and starting viewpoint that a person wants to investigate.

Vance Nelson, State Historical Society of North Dakota; historian, Fort Abercrombie State Historical Site.

Over the years, I have tried to balance my reading between books that will generally tell the military side of things and books that try to provide perspectives on the Native American viewpoints.

As I have think about the question of what *one* book most influenced my thinking on the Indian wars in the Great Plains, I still have a great deal of difficulty because there are so many books out there, and more are constantly being published that relate to the subject in one way or another. Each of them have a point of contribution to the overall understanding of the era.

The one book my wife Karen and I used to help get our children involved with an understanding of our work as interpreters at the former frontier military posts that are now in the National Park system, various state park or historical society systems, and city park systems, is entitled *Cricket, A Little Girl of the Old West*, by Helen Cooper Hooker. This author, we later discovered, wrote several books for children in a similar vein, and she did the majority of her work in writing these books at the post library at Fort Sill, Oklahoma. There are stories that tweak the heartstrings of sadness, stimulate hilarity, and provide a good general perspective of frontier military life and its special relationship to the U.S. government's policy toward Native American peoples. The storied create an avid interest in the West for both children *and* adults that will be the launching pad for further exploration.

The exploration of these interests through reading the many biographies of soldiers and Native Americans; general histories; histories of specific battles, forts, or units (military or tribal); histories of uniforms, accouterments, regalia, and fighting techniques can lead to a lifetime pursuit of knowledge. This pursuit continually sparks an interest for the need to do further research to try to find the answers to a multitude of questions, and that research leads to more writings.

It is sort of like trying to find the best swimming pool in the world to dive into. If you spend all of your time looking, you'll never get wet. Just dive in, experience, and enjoy, and then go find the next one to try out. Every swimmer in the pool might experience things a bit differently, depending upon the background brought into the pool, and their activity while in the pool, but it is the adventure of swimming that counts. So it is with reading all of the books (or as many as possible) on the Indian wars of the Great Plains.

C. Lee Noyes, New York, editor for the Custer Battlefield Historical and Museum Association.

The vast literature on the Indian wars includes many worthy candidates for this honor. However, one contribution to this genre is in a class by itself: Don Rickey's *Forty Miles a Day on Beans and Hay*. Several reasons compel the choice of this exemplary work that has stood the test of time. Although diaries and other primary sources have since further documented the daily life of the enlisted man in the post Civil War frontier army, they have not challenged Rickey's observations or his methodology. They have simply confirmed them. This realistic assessment remains an indispensable resource for all who share an interest in the Frontier Regulars regardless of knowledge and expertise. Rickey's seminal work successfully combines effective research and writing—a rare blend of such skills. The book's lucid prose and logical organization retain the attention of both the casual reader and the serious scholar. By successfully appealing to a broad audience, the author has ensured that the legacy of the frontier army and the life of the ordinary soldier have not been relegated to "the cold pages of the history books." *Forty Miles a Day on Beans and Hay* should be the nucleus of any library on the Indian Wars.

Jerry L. Russell, Arkansas, Chairman, Order of the Indian Wars/

The subject of white-Indian warfare during the settlement of the part of the North American continent that became the United States of America has held great interest for me for as long as I can remember. "Cowboys and Indians" was a favorite childhood game, and it was not till my introduction (through actor John Ford and film director John Wayne) that it was far more often "soldiers and Indians" than "cowboys and Indians." But after riding around Monument Valley [the landscape used by John Ford] many Saturday afternoons, I, reasonably enough, began to believe that "we" were the "good guys" and the Indians were the "bad guys." Not even *The Last of the Mohicans* and similar books shook my convictions about the "good guys" and the "bad guys."

But as I grew older and my awareness of the world and of history broadened, I began to understand that there might be more to the story of the Indian wars than I had come to believe. Which brings us up to 1970. And the year a broader analysis of Indian Wars history came on the scene through the publication of my favorite Indian wars book: *Bury My Heart at Wounded Knee: An Indian History of the American West*, by Dee Alexander Brown.

For me, and for millions of other readers of this book, a light bulb came on in my room of knowledge-beliefs-opinions about the red and white conflicts since the settling of the Jamestown colony in the early 17th century. It wasn't that John Ford and John Wayne had been wrong, or that James Fenimore Cooper had a corner on the truth; it was just that there was a lot more to the history of frontier conflicts than I had ever realized.

Basing his book on an extensive collection of Indian "speeches" that he had gathered over a long period of time, Brown set out to write a book for younger readers on Indian-white relations. But his literary agent pushed Brown to broaden his vision, and produce a book for readers of all ages.

Suddenly, other voices were heard in the historiographical conversations about the Indian Wars . . . Indian voices. Brown didn't attempt to say that all Indian versions were true and all white versions were false. In my mind, he simply offered historical views from a specific perspective, much as we had, before that time, mostly considered historical views from another perspective, thus broadening the opportunities for discussion and analysis. This process, I suppose, could, in weightiness, be considered "a search for the truth," which is, I hope what we are all after in our study of history.

Bury My Heart At Wounded Knee exploded like a bombshell into Indian wars history, exciting zealots on both sides, when it was only intended as an effort toward balance and is best approached from that perspective. But anyone who has an interest in Indian wars history is missing an irreplaceable part of the overall puzzle if *Bury My Heart At Wounded Knee* is not at least in the library of your mind.

Blair Stonechild, professor of Indian studies at Saskatchewan Indian Federated College; coauthor (with Bill Waiser) *Loyal Till Death: Indians and the North-West Rebellion* (a finalist candidate for the 1997 Governor General's Literary Award for Non-Fiction).

Loyal Till Death is a retrospective look at Indian involvement in the North-West Rebellion (1885) in western Canada. I was motivated to write by curiosity about the diametrically opposite accounts of Indian involvement and guilt between [the accounts of] Indian elders and official government accounts. *Loyal Till Death* uncovers an agenda of government conspiracy to blame and recriminate Indians. The Social Darwinist thinking of the time was clearly evident in the arrogant and demeaning attitudes of whites towards Indian motives and actions at the time. A resistance movement of the Métis led by Louis Riel was quickly transformed into a medium for the suppression of Indians during the final years of the Canadian frontier. Heavy handed measures taken by the federal government included the imprisonment of principal Indian leaders, despite indications of their loyalty, and the hanging of eight Indians in what was Canada's largest mass hanging. Oral history and archival research reveals a legacy of distrust of government and the need for significant measures to correct past injustices.

[*JIW* editor's note: Some United States readers may not be completely familiar with the North-West/Northwest Rebellion in Saskatchewan, although it was one of the largest conflicts involving persons of Indian descent in North American History. Blair Stonechild and Bill Waiser's book is part of an important debate on the nature and degree of participation by Indians, other than a few bands of Cree, in the conflict. Stonechild and Waiser conclude that the Canadian government exaggerated the extent of Indian involvement in order to impose repressive measures afterwards on the Western Indian nations. *Loyal Till Death* is also a ground breaking Canadian vindication of the value of Indian oral history, much as recent work in the United States has proven the worth of Indian testimony on the Great Sioux War of 1876.]

William Van Horn, researcher, U.S. Cavalry Memorial Library, Fort Riley, Kansas.

It's an interesting question: "What book most influenced your study of the Indian Wars?" My first response when asked for this issue was to cry, "Only one?" Quickly I ran down the list. Robert Utley's two volumes on the frontier army (classics!), John Bourke's *Campaigning with Crook*, Don Rickey's *Forty Miles a Day on Beans and Hay*. It just went on and on. Then it hit me.

For me, it would have to be Oliver Knight's *Life and Manners in the Frontier Army*. More than any other work, it turned my attention towards the men who wore blue on the plains. Like many, I'd seen the name of another author, Charles King before, mostly in connection with his book *Campaigning with Crook*. Although the bulk of King's work was fictional, it was heavily based on his service with the Fifth U.S. Cavalry. Knight's book was a revelation to me in more ways than one. For one thing, Knight made the factual basis of King's book clear. Knight's own book draws on both King's "fiction" and the memoirs of Old Army wives and officers to illustrate the many historically accurate elements in King's novels.

Reading *Life and Manners in the Frontier Army* changed the way I go about researching the Indian wars. For one thing, it made me very aware that not all the regular army regiments that served on the Plains had a biographer of the caliber of either King or the Custers (both the "Boy General" George A. Custer and his wife Elizabeth) to keep their memories alive. Having brought my attention to the way these soldiers lived, *Life and Manners* encouraged me to dig deeper, to find out just what these regiments did, both on and off campaign.

Knight's non-fiction writing naturally compliments King's fiction, drawing you fully into the world inhabited by these men and women after the Civil War. Knight pointed out some of the flaws, some of the internal censorship, that might have gone on in the memoirs published years later by army wives and some of their husbands. And then he draws on King's works to show what they might have left out. In his first chapters, Knight goes to great pains to show that King's work was fully appreciated and validated as authentic by the most important critics: his Old Army contemporaries. While avoiding any discussion of the literary merits of King's works, Knight approaches them as potential historical sources.

Knight's book was a heady combination of sources, and one that left me awed the first time I read it. Knight had opened a window into a world that many overlook. It actually swayed me to read some of King's novels for myself, discovering that they were as rich with information (and as predictably Victorian) as Knight suggests. With such a window into the Fifth Cavalry's parlor, I started looking for other windows into other regiments. Of the ten cavalry regiments on the Plains, only a bare handful has been examined in any detail. Knight's *Life and Manners in the Frontier Army* gave me that little push to start looking for more on the others.

Eliott West, professor of history, University of Arkansas, author of *Way to the West* and *The Contested Plains* (winner of the Ray Allen Billington Award of the Organization of American Historians).

No one comes close to Robert Utley in writing consistently excellent western military history. When I read *The Last Days of the Sioux Nation* in graduate school, it was a revelation: [a book] deeply researched and skillfully written and above all a model of how history can be all the more profoundly moving by being careful, professional, and balanced. Everything that Bob Utley has written since then has taught me (and all his readers) plenty, both in its content and through his example of a determination to get things right.

Three other works show a similar mingling of dogged research and fine writing. Paul Hutton's *Phil Sheridan and His Army* remains one of the finest single volumes in this very crowded field. As its title promises, it manages to combine biography with a vivid portrayal of the western military experience. *William Tecumseh Sherman and the Settlement of the West*, by my mentor Robert Athearn, similarly considers the Indian wars through the life an extraordinary- -and extraordinarily complicated—man, and it does so with animated writing and humor. In *Children of Grace*, Bruce Hampton shows an exceptional gift of fashioning from a mountain of sources a fast-moving narrative of arguably the most remarkable western Indian war: the Nez Perce conflict of 1877.

As a social historian, I remain mildly in awe of Don Rickey, Jr.'s *Forty Miles a Day on Beans and Hay*, with its dense description of army life and its unerring feel for the experience of common grunts in the field and in the barracks. For similar reasons, I admire greatly the writing of Sherry Smith. Her *The View From Officer's Row* takes us into the social and perceptual world of the western military, and it does so with a rare insight and sensitivity.

I suspect I am at odds with many colleagues—and I know I am with my friend Bob Utley—in also admiring Evan S. Connell's *Son of the Morning Star*. Yes, it is eccentric and disjointed, and occasionally bizarre readings of particular episodes betray a spotty understanding of a larger context, but Connell has a feel for the utter strangeness of Custer's West and a passion for the revealing detail. Odd as it is, it grows on you.

Finally, Peter John Powell's *People of the Sacred Mountain* shows us the native perspective of western military history, both conflicts among the various Indian peoples and those with their army adversaries. The stories are full of newly realized heroism, mystery, disaster and transcendence. To use a favorite phrase of a friend, you cannot read this book without rearranging your mental furniture.

NATIVE VOICES
There Are No Accidents

Clifford E. Trafzer

A few years ago the Native American Heritage Commission in California met with the U. S. Forest Service on Mt. Shasta to discuss preserving Panther Meadows, a holy place for Indian people of California and Oregon. As a state agency, the commission could not dictate policy to Forest, but we wanted them to know that many Native Americans opposed further development of *Ako-Yet*. I explained to one supervisor that native people believed that at the beginning of time the Creator a placed a great basket inside the mountain, a basket that sent positive blessings to the entire world. The forest supervisor took off his cap, scratched his head, and said, "I don't know about that, but if there is a basket with good vibs [sic] in there, it sure ain't doin a good job." I responded by asking the man to imagine a world without the basket.

The area around Mt. Shasta has been exploited by miners, merchants, cattlemen, lumber companies, tourist, and skiers. These people come and go, often ignoring native views about sacred places and important events. We know about native history through documents and oral history, although some historians discount oral history as illegitimate. One reviewer for my work on the Palouse Indians (*Renegade Tribe: The Palouse Indians and the Invasion of the Inland Pacific Northwest* [Lewiston: Washington State University Press, 1986]) told the University of Oklahoma Press that I must remove oral history from my manuscript, because as we all know, such history is "fish tales that grow with the telling." I took my manuscript elsewhere. Anthropologists, ethnologists, and linguists have listened and learned from Native Americans for years, but some historians have not. In part, historians have not listened because, to some scholars, oral history is suspect and unreliable. But it also takes a good deal of time to conduct oral histories, particularly among native communities where it is important to establish trust, a condition that takes time and expense.

In addition to doing my own oral histories in the Southwest, Northwest, California, and Oklahoma, I have relied on those taken by reputable people. While living on the Navajo Reservation, I interviewed various people about many topics related to Navajo history. I traveled into the Canyon del Muerto with members of the Draper family and listened to oral histories given by the Day and Damon families and their friends. I listened to my Navajo students and colleagues and learned. However, I also learned a great deal about the Kit Carson campaign and Navajo Long Walk from Ruth Roessell's classic Navajo Stories of the Long Walk Period. Ruth is Diné, speaks the language, and knew many of the people she interviewed. Her work and oral histories Navajos shared with me changed my research, interpretation, and way of thinking about the Navajo Wars.

When I took a position at Washington State University (WSU), I lived in the heart of the Palouse Country. I determined to research the Palouse Indians who had been forcefully removed from the region and, with the help of Richard Scheuerman, conducted oral interviews on the Yakama, Umatilla, Nez Perce, and Colville reservations. The research and interactions enriched my work, but so did my exploration of the McWhorter and Brown collections in the WSU Library. L. V. McWhorter's books, *Yellow Wolf* and *Here Me, My Chiefs!* changed my presentation of Northwestern Indian history because both books and McWhorter's collection allowed me to enter a past world filled with events that are difficult to interpret. McWhorter was a close friend of Yellow Wolf, and they traveled together to retrace the flight of Nez Perce and Palouse people in 1877. Yellow Wolf's keen memory, notes, and sketches became part of my own work, thanks to the record left in English by McWhorter and Alvin Josephy's *The Nez Perce Indians*—a masterful book that also drew on McWhorter's work.

In 1961, Judge William Brown published *The Indian Side of the Story*, a book that is filled with oral histories and native insights, a book generally ignored by historians. Brown interviewed many Indians, including family members of Chiefs Kamiakin and Owhi, by far the most important war leaders in the Northwest during the 1850s. Brown interviewed Owhi's daughter (Mary Moses) and others who participated in the turbulent years after 1853. His book and collection held keys to understanding the familial, band, and inter-tribal struggles of the late nineteenth century. These were the very topics still mentioned in the 1970s and 1980s by tribal elders Mary Jim, Emily Peone, Art Kamiakin, and Lucy Covington. All of these elders and others remained tied to their traditional spiritual beliefs, and these doctrines can be found in Click Relander's *Drummers and Dreamers* and the contemporary work of Robert Ruby and John Brown on Smohalla. Relander's book is unorganized and difficult to read, but like his collection at the Yakima Valley Regional Library, offers many insights that cannot be found elsewhere into native religion of Indians from the Columbia Plateau.

Contemporary tribal elders often remind me: "There are no accidents." They believe that it was no accident that Yellow Wolf brought a lame horse to McWhorter and began a life-long friendship. It was no accident that Judge Brown left a body of oral histories about the Plateau Indian War. And it is no accident that contemporary Chemehuevi, Serrano, Cahuilla, Kumeyaay, Luiseño, and Quechan people in California share their oral histories with me today. They are purposely providing researchers a body of information so that we may enter their worlds and learn from their own mothers and fathers, aunts and uncles, grandmothers and grandfathers. They want academics to hear and use their voices, thoughts, ideas, and beliefs so that we may come to appreciate their diverse people, families, communities, and cultures. Historians and historiography of the Indian wars and related fields will be more informed by gathering, assessing, and critically analyzing native voices found in past volumes and in our own body of research shared by contemporary native people.

We would all do well to listen and learn from native voices.

By Glint of Lantern Late
The Texts of Custer and the Cadets

Rodney G. Thomas

The movers came quietly that summer morning of 1876. With heartfelt grief and respect for the lady of the house, the detail of soldiers moved with muffled efficiency. Mrs. George Armstrong Custer was leaving Fort Abraham Lincoln, Dakota Territory. She, like the other widows newly created by a battle far away on the Little Bighorn, was packing a long trip back to the civilian world. Fort Abraham Lincoln would not see the likes of her or her husband for a long time to come. As the soldiers entered the study of the officer's quarters, one of them noted that they would need several strong crates just to hold the books. Two days later the moving detail left as quietly as it had come. All the Custer belongings—clothes, stuffed trophy animals, guns, piano, and books—were gone. All the books read by glint of lantern late had been carefully packed to accompany the widow Custer on her long journey.

Books? Could such a library have belonged to the most famous man ever to hold the position of "last man in his class" at the U.S. Military Academy? Yet the scenario above is not a fantasy. A famous photograph of George and Libby Custer shows them in that very study surrounded by stuffed animals, weapons, and yes... books. Lots of books.[1] What might he have read—or failed to read?

This article has two purposes. The first is to identify the standard texts read in the nineteenth century by academy trained officers such as Custer. The second goal is to reexamine the common assertion that the U.S. Army had no adequate doctrine for battling Indian forces, and that this explains many of its failures in the West. Identifying the books that once dominated military education in the United States can be difficult. Many of the volumes have sat

George Custer posed for this picture with his wife Libbie and a former runaway slave Eliza Brown three days after the Confederate surrender at Appomattox Court House. *CBNM*

unused and forgotten on dusty shelves for decades. Also, those familiar with them often did not directly cite the titles as they would today. Instead, an author often referred vaguely to works containing "doctrine of the times." There would often be no indication of what that doctrine was or in which book(s) it might be described. But however vague the references, they do indicate that the Army early on developed tactical and strategic concepts, and that it believed those concepts could be taught using required texts.

At the end of the American Revolution in 1783, the United States scarcely possessed an army, much less an institution at which to teach its future officers. With the coming of peace, the Army was reduced to eighty soldiers assigned to guard stores at West Point, New York. Had it not been for internal "revolts" over taxation and foreclosures (the Whiskey Revolt and Shay's Rebellion) and frontier altercations with the British and Indians, that little garrison might have been discharged as well. For the next ninety years, the military was primarily concerned with civil tasks such as exploring and surveying, and with guarding an expanding frontier. One fight on the frontier in 1791, the Arthur St. Clair debacle on the banks of the Wabash River, resulted in the Army losing 623 killed and 258 wounded. It was the single largest defeat ever inflicted on the Army by Indian forces.

The defeat of St. Clair's ill-trained and poorly led officers and men was perhaps a factor in the founding of the United States Military Academy at West Point in 1802. With the establishment of West Point, the Army established a process for creating officers with professional credentials and created an intellectual foundation for its decision making. Cadets at the academy were, while working on degrees in engineering, to be exposed to doctrine based on European and nascent American military thought.

At the time West Point was opened, European authors dominated military textbooks. References studied in the United States from the 1700s until the 1840s were generally British or English translations of French or German works. They included Colonel Frederick Herrier's *Abstract of Colonel Herrier's Instructions for Volunteer Corps of Cavalry*, published in 1811; Robert Hewes's *An Elucidation of Regulations for the Formations and Movements of Cavalry*, dated 1804, which copied a British manual of the same name though with a different foreword; and an 1802 British manual reprinted in Boston, *Rules and Regulations for the Sword Exercise of the Cavalry to Which is Added the Review Exercise*. The main theoretical military art and science reference used until the 1840s was Edwin Hoyt's *A Treatise on the Military Art in Four Parts*, published in Brattleborough, Vermont, in 1798.

By the close of the Mexican War in 1848, the Army had not only defeated its Mexican equivalent but also most of the Indian forces arrayed against it east of the Mississippi. These victories were achieved by a nation whose doctrinal underpinnings were still largely influenced by Europeans. However, more military texts had been produced in the United States since the 1820s. Some of the most commonly used American titles used in training in the 1820s through 1840s were Samuel Cooper's *A Concise System of Instructions and Regulations for the Militia and Volunteers of the United States*, published in 1836 and reprinted in 1847; *A System of Tactics, or, Rules for the Exercises and Maneuvers of the Cavalry and Light Infantry and Riflemen of the United States*, published in 1834; and William T. Tone's *School of Cavalry; or, System of Organization, Instruction, and Maneuvers, Proposed for the Cavalry of the United States*, published in 1824.

The books that were perhaps the most influential in forming nineteenth century U.S. cavalry doctrine were published in 1841. These were the three volumes of J. R. Poinsett's *Cavalry Tactics: First Part. School of the*

Trooper—Of the Platoon and of the Squadron—Dismounted. The volumes were reprinted in 1855, 1861, and 1862 by private publishers.. In 1864, the Government Printing Office in Washington for the War reprinted them, establishing their contents as "official" Army doctrine. The tactics and methodologies Poinsett expounded were then used almost exclusively for training cavalry units. The cavalry organization, tactics, and maneuvers taught in publications throughout the 1870s and 1880s all drew wholly or in significant part on Poinsett's works. As George Custer graduated from West Point in 1861, his formal training in cavalry tactics would likely have been based on Poinsett. Meanwhile, artillery doctrine was centered on Alfred Mordecai's *Artillery for the Land Service of the United States*, published in 1848. With few exceptions Mordecai's instruction guided artillery instruction for the next 40 or so years.

Following the conclusion of the Mexican War in 1818, the Army's responsibilities largely shifted west of the Mississippi River into what was popularly known in those days as "The Great American Desert." In this postwar period, European texts were still read in the United States. But there had been no conflicts in Europe since the Napoleonic wars significant enough to force a change in traditional thinking. As a result, texts inspired by the campaigns of Napoleon, such as those by Baron Antoni Jomini, did not enjoy their former popularity in the United States. Instead, American military thought after 1848 centered on the works of the Mahan brothers, one of whom was in the Army and the other in the Navy. Captain D. H. Mahan's *Advanced-Guard, Out-Post, and Detachment Service of Troops, with the Essential Principles of Strategy and Grand Tactics for the Use of Officers of the Militia and Volunteers* was first published in 1847 and was revised and reprinted in 1863. It contained the first serious American military theoretical thought and remained unsurpassed in influence until the early 1900s. Major Henry W. Halleck's *Elements of Military Art and Science*, which had preceded Mahan's book by a year, was not as well received. Halleck would during the Civil War be considered a plodder, and the difficulties posed by his text seemed to predict that.

Another milestone was the 1855 publication of Captain William J. Hardee's celebrated *Light Infantry Tactics*. Hardee compiled his book almost from *A System of Tactics, or, Rules for the Exercises and Maneuvers of the Cavalry and Light Infantry and Riflemen of the United States*, published in 1834. Unlike his source, Hardee's book would see several reprints, and it is today one of the better known period texts. The "Hardee System" of infantry operation would remain the one of choice for infantry units until 1867. In that year it was finally superseded by Brevet Major General Emory Upton's *New System of Infantry Tactics* (revised in 1874 as *Infantry Tactics Double and Single Rank Adapted to American Topography and Improved Firearms*). Upton's text remained the standard on infantry until 1891.

The American Civil War (1861-1865) created a most hurried need for training publications and other printed military information. This inspired the production of several texts by well known military figures of the time. These included works such as Brigadier General Phillip St. George Cooke's *Cavalry Tactics: Or, Regulations for the Instruction, Formations, and Movements of the Army and Volunteers of the United States*. Secretary of War Simon Cameron authorized the printing of *Cavalry Tactics* on 1 November 1861, less than six months after the war began (although the forwarding letter from Cooke was dated 11 January 1860). Cooke's *Tactics* was twice reprinted and remained the official U. S. Army cavalry manual until 1874. As was the case with infantry manuals, it was Emory Upton who replaced the standard cavalry text. In 1874, Upton published a revision of Cooke's work that he entitled *Cavalry Tactics: United States Army Assimilated to the Tactics of Infantry and Artillery*. (However, Upton's cavalry system had already been officially adopted in General Orders Number 6 of 17 July 1873.) Upton's *Tactics* remained the standard manual until 1887. Besides the works of Mahan, Hardee, and Cooke, there were a plethora of hastily written texts by other lesser figures that were supposed to guide units and leaders in their prosecution of the Civil War. Most of these works were heavily derivative of, or even thinly disguised copies, of the works discussed above.

It would be easy to suppose, based on the sheer quantity of publications, that the Civil War produced a rich harvest of improvements in doctrine and training as far as textbooks were concerned. Unfortunately this was not the case. If anything, the Army returned to the Western frontier even more entrenched in traditional thinking. Fighting intense warfare for four years using the methodology and tactics taught in the textbooks did not adequately prepare the Army for the next round of battles and skirmishes with Indian forces.

However, were all of the Army's problems out West caused by outmoded training and information? It is often said the Army did not develop, teach, or publish a doctrine for fighting Indians. Alternately, it is stated that there was a doctrine but that it was not adequate for the type of warfare acquired. There are two problems with these conclusions. The first difficulty is that they are based on the assumption that officers remembered what they read and were taught and that they always applied those teachings correctly. From the author's personal experience, he can testify that reading standard military texts is a daunting task not often aided by any writing style approaching that of a Hemingway. The way doctrinal texts are written is often as dry as a high plains desert in August. It is not, in other words, as memorable as it is essential. To an officer a decade or more out of West Point, as many were on the Frontier, what they were taught would have been all the more forgettable. In addition, there was seldom cause to remember instruction on a frequent basis. Western garrison duty might produce a month of tedium for every one day of applied tactics.

When officers did see action, they made some of their worst blunders when they misapplied or disregarded traditional texts and training. The Dakota Sioux Uprising of 1862 and the 1876 campaigns of the Great Sioux War provide good examples. In the former, one command was virtually annihilated at Redwood Ferry when it failed to carry out reconnaissance—despite reports of attacks nearby. At Birch Coulee, an even better forewarned command was surrounded when it failed to post enough guards. In both instances, poorly trained soldiers paid the price when inexperienced officers ignored conventional doctrine. At the Little Bighorn in 1876, Custer was certainly not unique in underestimating his opponents. But repetitive splitting of forces in the face of an unknown enemy defied everything he had ever been taught. In both of these conflicts, a lack of doctrine or inadequate doctrine was certainly not the problem. Also, as George Crook found out at the Battle of the Rosebud a few weeks before Custer's last battle, sometimes the problem was not doctrine but simply being outfought by the Indians.

The other problem with assuming that the Army's problem was outmoded information is that useful texts were actually available. There probably was a lack on "official" guidance on prosecuting warfare against Indians. But frontier army officers had access to a significant body of useful information. Newspapers such as *The Army-Navy Journal* (1866-1916), the *Army-Navy Register* and the dailies and weeklies of major cities were read regularly on military posts. These papers and journals, such as the *Galaxy, Atlantic Monthly, Harpers*, and *Scribner's* often published news, analyses, and interviews concerning the Indian frontier. Published memoirs such as Lawrence Kip's *Army Life on the Pacific: A Journal of the Expedition Against the Northern Indians in the Summer of 1858* (1859), Randolph March's *Thirty Years of Army Life on the Border* (1866) and John C. Cremony's *Life Among the Apaches* (1868) gave firsthand accounts of frontier campaigning. Custer himself was a well-known and respected raconteur of Army life and war on the frontier, with several publications to his credit.

Did Custer himself read all those books? The question may have been answered by a chance discovery in 1954. A note dated January 17, 1887, signed by Lt. E. A. Garlington and addressed to Mrs. George A. Custer, bears witness that he probably did. In language as terse and official as only an officer can write, Garlington stated: "It is the policy of this post to provide the best in literature and history for all occupants to peruse. Your husband withdrew from the post library the following books and they have not been returned. Should you know of the whereabouts of these books please return them to the Library of this Post." The note was hidden in the volumes until they and the other books packed by the soldiers in July 1876 were found in the Custer family farmhouse.

NOTES

1. Lawrence A. Frost. "Two Sides of a General," in *Custer and His Times, Book 3.* Edited by Gregory J. W. Urwin and Roberta E. Fagan (Conway: University of Central Arkansas Press and the Little Big Horn Associates, 1987), 121-147.

Jerry L. Russell, Founder and National Chairman

THE STUDY OF THE MILITARY HISTORY of the early settlement of North America, and the continuing conflicts between Indian and Indian, Indian and settler, Indian and soldier, has long been a subject that has fascinated succeeding generations of Americans.

In the early decades of this century, an organization known as **The Order of Indian Wars of the United States**, made up primarily of retired military men, actual veterans of the Indian Wars, devoted its attention to the study of the U.S. military establishment's role in the development and settlement of this country's westward-moving frontier. That organization became an affiliate of the American Military Institute in 1947, and is once again active for descendants.

IN 1979, WE FOUNDED A **NEW** ORGANIZATION, inspired by that other group—a "spiritual descendant," if you will—but having no connection, official or otherwise with the predecessor. Our purpose, however, is similar—but broader: the in-depth study and dissemination of information on America's frontier conflicts. We are as interested in the "Indian side" as in the "Army/settlers side," although this organization, and its Assemblies, are not to be a forum for political or sociological crusades or guilt trips—our interest is in **military history**.

An additional purpose, equally important, we believe, is our concern for the historic preservation of those important sites associated with the history of the Indian Wars in America. Citizens' groups must become more involved in historic preservation, or much of our past will be irretrievably lost, in the name of 'progress'. Historic military sites are an important part of our national heritage, and the preservation/protection of these sites will be a major, continuing, concern of our organization—hence our motto: WE WHO STUDY MUST ALSO STRIVE TO SAVE! HERITAGEPAC is the national lobbying organization established in 1989 to work for preservation of battlesites. Our main publication is the *OIW Communique*.

DUES ARE $20 A YEAR

CUSTER & THE LITTLE BIG HORN

Our 23rd Annual Assembly will focus on the 125th Anniversary of the Battle of the Little Big Horn. We will meet in Sheridan, Wyoming, June 21-24, 2001, with tours of the
Battle of the Rosebud and the Little Big Horn Campaign.

WRITE FOR INFORMATION
Order of the Indian Wars
P.O. Box 7401, Little Rock AR 72217
501-225-3996   Send Postal Address to <indianwars@aristotle.net>

Recommended Reading

The Fifteen Greatest North American Indian Wars

The fifteen "wars" or series of wars discussed in this article were, by number of participants, the fifteen greatest conflicts in the history of the present-day United States and the Canadian borderland. These wars date from the late seventeenth century—late in the European colonial period—to the end of the nineteenth century. Isolated incidents that were not part of sustained hostilities are not included. For example, the lists exclude the fighting that took place during Francisco Vasquez de Coronado's and Hernando de Soto's expeditions in the sixteenth century. Likewise, early colonial wars that involved a high percentage of an Indian or European population but not the sheet numbers involved in later conflicts are also omitted. For this reason, the list does not include events such as Metacom's War ("King Philip's War") in the seventeenth century or the many Indian hostilities that took place coincident with Queen Anne's War in the early eighteenth century.

The United States War Department and the U.S. Congress "officially determined" that twelve "Indian campaigns approaching the magnitude of wars" took place between 1865 and 1900. These distinctions were made to determine which soldiers had the right to wear "service in war" uniform chevrons and to receive war service pensions. (House Report No. 1084, 63rd Congress, 2nd Session, Vol. 3, 1913, Serial 6560, "Pensions for Indian War Veterans"). One conflict covered in the reading lists, the Bozeman Trail War (1867-1868), were excluded from the government's list of wars despite the high number of men and engagements involved. Conversely, five of the "official"

Indian wars are not covered in the readings lists as they did not reach the scale of the top fifteen events. These five excluded conflicts are the:

1) "Campaigns in southern Oregon and Idaho and northern parts of California and Nevada, 1865-1868" (principally the conflict known as the Paiute War, sometimes ambiguously termed the "Snake War," 1866-1868);
2) "Modoc War, 1872 and 1873";
3) "Bannock War [or Bannock-Paiute War], 1878";
4) "Campaign against the Ute Indians in Colorado and Utah, September, 1879, to November, 1880" (principally the White River Expedition, 1879);
5) "Campaign against the Sioux Indians in South Dakota, November, 1890, to January, 1891" (the "Wounded Knee Campaign" or "Pine Ridge Campaign").

The British government also made an official determination of which were its "wars" in North America; these included the Northwest Rebellion of 1885. The Northwest Rebellion was "officially" fought against the Métis, a distinct prairie population of mixed French-Indian descent. The number of Indians in arms was relatively small. Special recognition for participation in the Northwest Rebellion was essentially restricted to those British and Canadians who had been in expeditions against the Métis versus those who marched against Cree combatants. However, the aggregate of troops sent in pursuit of the participating Indians would make the Northwest Rebellion one of the largest Indian wars of North America. For this reason, the conflict is covered below in an addenda.

Most works listed below are *secondary* works that can be appreciated by the average history buff. A few well annotated or easily followed collections of primary sources are also included. Books that would appeal largely to researchers or to the more serious students of campaigns are noted separately. Usually the most recent hard cover editions of titles are provided, though some works are currently available only in soft cover editions.

1. *French and Indian War, 1754-1763, (including the Anglo-Cherokee War of 1759-1761) and Pontiac's War/Uprising, 1763-1764*

Jennings, Francis, *Empire of Fortune: Crowns, Colonies and Tribes in the Seven Years' War in America* (New York, 1988).

Kopperman, Paul, *Braddock at the Monongahela* (Pittsburgh, 1976). OP

William R. Nester's *"Haughty Conquerors:" Amherst and the Great Indian Uprising of 1763* (Westport, 2000).

Peckham, Howard, *Pontiac and the Indian Uprising* (Detroit, 1994).

Sipe, C. Hale, *The Indian Wars of Pennsylvania: French and Indian War, Pontiac's War, Lord Dunmore's War, the Revolutionary War and the Indian Uprisings from 1789 to 1795*, 2nd ed. (Lewisburg, 1994).

Waddell, Louis and Bruce Bomberger, *The French and Indian Wars in Pennsylvania, 1753-1763: Fortification and Struggle During the War for Empire* (Harrisburg Pennsylvania Historical and Museum Commission, 1996). [A short publication.]

See also specific chapters of:

Anderson, Fred, *Crucible of War: The Seven Years' War and the Fate of Empire in British North America, 1754-1766* (New York, 2000).

Calloway, Colin G., *The Western Abenakis of Vermont, 1600-1800: War, Migration, and the Survival of an Indian People* (Norman, 1990).

Corkran, David H., *The Cherokee Frontier* (Norman, 1962). OP

Ferling, John E., *A Wilderness of Miseries: War and Warriors in Early America* (Westport, 1980).

Steele, Ian K., *Warpaths: Invasions of North America* (New York, 1994).

Important related books and specialized books:

West, J. Martin, ed., *War for Empire in Western Pennsylvania* (Ligonier, PA: Fort Ligonier Association, 1993). [A short publication.]

Hunger, William A., *Forts on the Pennsylvania Frontier, 1753-1758* (1960; reprint, Lewisburg, PA: Wennawoods Publishing, 1999).

Steele, Ian K., *Betrayals: Fort William Henry and the Massacre* (New York: Oxford University Press, 1990)

Van de Water, Frederic F., *Lake Champlain and Lake George* (1946; reprint, Port Washington, NY: Associated Faculty Press, 1969).

[Nester's *"Haughty Conquerors"* is included on the basis of the publisher's description, as it appears to be one of the only two book-length treatments of Pontiac's War in this century—it has not yet been read or reviewed by anyone associated with *JIW*. While noting that no person thanked either endorsed or disparaged any titles, *JIW* acknowledges the assistance of bibliographies or book lists produced by staff members of Bushy Run Battlefield State Historic Site, Pennsylvania; Eastern National; Fort Ligonier [Museum], Ligonier, PA; Fort Necessity National Battlefield; Fort Pitt Museum at Point State Park, Pennsylvania; New York State Office of Parks, Recreation and Historic Preservation; Pennsylvania Historical and Museum Commission; Pennsylvania Military Museum. Thanks also to Ted Alexander.]

2. *Indian Wars of the War of American Independence or American Revolution, 1775-1783; (preceded by Lord Dunmore's War, 1774, and including the Chickamauga Cherokee Wars, 1779-1780, 1786, 1788-1789)*

Bakeless, John, *Background to Glory: The Life of George Rogers Clark* (1957; reprint, Lincoln: University of Nebraska Press, 1992).

Eckert, Allan W., *That Dark and Bloody River: Chronicles of the Ohio River Valley* (New York: Bantam Books, 1995).

Graymont, Barbara, *The Iroquois in the American Revolution* (Syracuse: Syracuse University Press, 1972).

Harrison, Lowell Hayes, *George Rogers Clark and the War in the West* (1976; reprint, Lexington: University Press of Kentucky, 2001).

Mintz, Max M., *Seeds of Empire: The American Revolutionary Conquest of the Iroquois* (New York: New York University Press, 1999.)

O'Donnell, James H., *Southern Indians in the American Revolution*, 3rd ed. (Knoxville: University of Tennessee Press, 1973).

Sipe, C. Hale, *The Indian Wars of Pennsylvania: French and Indian War, Pontiac's War, Lord Dunmore's War, the Revolutionary War and the Indian Uprisings from 1789 to 1795*, 2nd ed. (1931; reprint, Lewisburg, PA: Wennawoods Publishing, 1994).

See also specific chapters of:
Dowd, Gregory Evans, *A Spirited Resistance: The North American Indian Struggle for Unity, 1745-1815* (Baltimore: Johns Hopkins University Press, 1992.)

Downes, Randolph C., *Council Fires on the Upper Ohio: A Narrative of Indian Affairs in the Upper Ohio Valley until 1795* (Pittsburgh: University of Pittsburgh Press, 1940). [Out of print.]

Driver, Carl S., *John Sevier: Pioneer of the Old Southwest* (Chapel Hill: University of North Carolina, 1932). [Out of print.]

Fischer, Joseph R., *A Well-Executed Failure The Sullivan Campaign Against the Iroquois, July-September, 1779* (Columbia: University of South Carolina Press, 1997).

Flexner, James Thomas, *Mohawk Baronet: Sir William Johnson of New York* (1959; reprint, Syracuse, NY: Syracuse University Press, 1989).

Kelsay, Isabel Thompson, *Joseph Brant, 1743-1807: Man of Two Worlds* (Syracuse: Syracuse University Press, 1984).

Hurt, R. Douglas, *The Ohio Frontier: Crucible of the Old Northwest, 1720-1830* (Bloomington: Indiana University Press, 1996).

Whittemore, Charles Park, *A General of the Revolution: John Sullivan of New Hampshire* (New York: Columbia University Press, 1961). [Out of print.]

Important related books an specialized books:

Barnhart, John D., ed., *Henry Hamilton and George Rogers Clark in the American Revolution* (Crawfordsville, IN: R. E. Banta, 1951). [Out of print.]

Calloway, Colin G., *The American Revolution in Indian Country: Crisis and Diversity in Native American Communities* (New York: Cambridge University Press, 1995).

Lewis, Virgil Anson, *History of the Battle of Point Pleasant, Fought Between White Men and Indians at the Mouth of the Great Kanawha River (Now Point Pleasant, West Virginia)* (1909; reprint, Harrisonburg, VA: C. J. Carrier Company, 1974).

Mohr, Walter H., *Federal Indian Relations, 1774-1788* (Philadelphia: University of Pennsylvania Press, 1933). [Out of print.]

Swiggett, Howard, *War Out of Niagara: Walter Butler and the Tory Rangers* (1933; reprint, Port Washington, NY: I. J. Friedman, 1961).

[There are no comprehensive works on American Indians in the American Revolution, though there are several good regional and ethnic studies. Lewis's book on the Battle of Point Pleasant is dated but one of the few available sources on Lord Dunmore's War. While noting that no person thanked either endorsed or disparaged any titles, *JIW* acknowledges the assistance of bibliographies or book lists produced by staff members of Eastern National; Fort Stanwix National Monument; George Rogers Clark National Historical Park; Indiana

Historical Bureau; Kentucky Historical Society; Kentucky Military History Museum; New York State Office of Parks, Recreation and Historic Preservation; Sycamore Shoals State Historic Area, Tennessee; Tennessee Historical Commission.]

3. *War in the Old Northwest, 1783-1795 (including the "Miami War" or Little Turtle's War, 1790-1795)*

Eckert, Allan W., *That Dark and Bloody River: Chronicles of the Ohio River Valley* (New York: Bantam Books, 1995).
Jacobs, James Ripley, *The Beginning of the U.S. Army, 1783-1812* (1947; reprint, Westport, CT: Greenwood Press, 1977).
Sugden, John, *Blue Jacket: Warrior of the Shawnees* (Lincoln: University of Nebraska press, 2000).
Sword, Wiley, *President Washington's Indian War: The Struggle for the Old Northwest, 1790-1795* (Norman: University of Oklahoma Press, 1985).

See also specific chapters of:

Anson, Bert, *The Miami Indians* (Norman: University of Oklahoma press, 1970).
Dowd, Gregory Evans, *A Spirited Resistance: The North American Indian Struggle for Unity, 1745-1815* (Baltimore: Johns Hopkins University Press, 1992).
Downes, Randolph C., *Council Fires on the Upper Ohio: A Narrative of Indian Affairs in the Upper Ohio Valley until 1795* (Pittsburgh: University of Pittsburgh Press, 1940). [Out of print.]
Eckert, Allan W., *That Dark and Bloody River: Chronicles of the Ohio River Valley* (New York: Bantam Books, 1995).
Edmunds, R. David, *The Potawatomis: Keepers of the Fire* (Norman: University of Oklahoma Press, 1978).
Hurt, R. Douglas, *The Ohio Frontier: Crucible of the Old Northwest, 1720-1830* (Bloomington: Indiana University Press, 1996).
Nelson, Paul David, *Anthony Wayne, Soldier of the Early Republic* (Bloomington: Indiana University Press, 1985).

Prucha, Francis Paul, *The Sword of the Republic: The United States Army on the Frontier, 1783-1846* (1969; reprint, in paper Lincoln: University of Nebraska Press, 1969).

Important related books and specialized books:

Clifton, James A., *The Prairie People: Continuity and Change in Potowatomi Indian Culture, 1663-1965* (Iowa City: University of Iowa Press, 1977, 1998).

Edel, Wilbur, *Kekionga!: The Worst Defeat in the History of the U.S. Army* (Westport, CT: Praeger, 1997).

[Edel's *Kekionga!* is included on the basis of the publisher's description, as it appears to be the only book-length treatment of the defeat of Gen. Josiah Harmar's 1790 expedition; it has not been read or reviewed by anyone associated with *JIW*. While noting that no person thanked either endorsed or disparaged any titles, *JIW* acknowledges the assistance of bibliographies or book lists produced by staff members of the Allen County-Fort Wayne (Indiana) Historical Society; the Heidelberg College Center for Historical and Military Archeology; the Indiana Historical Society; and the Ohio Historical Society.]

4. *Tecumseh's Resistance, 1809-1811; Creek War of 1813-1814; and War of 1812, 1812-1815*

Antal, Sandy, *A Wampum Denied: Proctor's War of 1812* (Ottawa: Carleton University Press; East Lansing, MI: Michigan State University Press, 1997).

Gilpin, Alec R., *The War of 1812 in the Old Northwest* (East Lansing: Michigan State University Press, 1958). [Out of print.]

Griffith, Benjamin W., Jr., *McIntosh and Weatherford, Creek Indian Leaders* (reprint, University: University of Alabama Press, 1998).

Remini, Robert V., *Andrew Jackson and His Indian Wars* (New York: Viking Press, forthcoming in 2001).

Sugden, John, *Tecumseh: A Life* (New York: Henry Holt, 1999).

See also specific chapters of:

The Death of Tecumseh in 1813 at the Battle of the Thames. *LC*

Cleaves, Freeman, *Old Tippecanoe: William Henry Harrison and His Time* (reprint, Newtown, CT: American Political Biography Press, 1990).

Dowd, Gregory Evans, *A Spirited Resistance: The North American Indian Struggle for Unity, 1745-1815* (1939; Baltimore: Johns Hopkins University Press, 1992).

Owsley, Frank Lawrence, *Struggle for the Gulf Borderlands The Creek War and the Battle of New Orleans, 1812-1815* (1981; reprint, Tuscaloosa: University of Alabama Press, 2000).

Prucha, Francis Paul, *The Sword of the Republic: The United States Army on the Frontier, 1783-1846* (1969; reprint in paper, Lincoln: University of Nebraska Press, 1969).

Important related books and specialized books:

Allen, Robert S., *His Majesty's Indian Allies: British Indian Policy in the Defense of Canada* (Toronto: Dundurn Press, 1992).

Benn, Carl, *The Iroquois in the War of 1812* (Toronto: University of Toronto Press, 1998).

Edmunds, R. David, *The Shawnee Prophet* (Lincoln: University of Nebraska Press, 1983).

———, *Tecumseh and the Quest for Indian Leadership* (Boston: Little, Brown, 1984).

Halbert, Henry S. and T. H. Ball, *The Creek War of 1813 and 1814* (1895; reprint, Tuscaloosa: University of Alabama Press, 1995).

[While noting that no person thanked either endorsed or disparaged any titles, *JIW* acknowledges the assistance of bibliographies or book lists produced by staff members of Eastern National; Fort Malden National Historical Park, Parks Canada; Horseshoe Bend National Military Park; Indiana Historical Bureau; Ohio Historical Society; and the Tippecanoe County (Indiana) Historical Society. Thanks also to John Alden Reid.].

5. *Black Hawk War, 1832*

Eby, Cecil, *"That Disgraceful Affair," the Black Hawk War* (New York: W.W. Norton, 1973).

Hagan, William T., *The Sac and Fox Indians* (Norman: University of Oklahoma Press, 1958).

See also sSpecific chapters of:

Bauer, K. Jack, *Zachary Taylor: Soldier, Planter, Statesman of the Old Southwest.* (1985; Baton Rouge: Louisiana State University Press, 1993)

Nichols, Roger L., *General Henry Atkinson: A Western Military Career* (Norman: University of Oklahoma Press, 1965). [Out of print.]

Prucha, Francis Paul, *The Sword of the Republic: The United States Army on the Frontier, 1783-1846* (1969; reprint, in paper Lincoln: University of Nebraska Press, 1969).

Important related books and specialized books:

Jackson, Donald, ed., *Black Hawk: An Autobiography* (published as *Life of Ma-ka-tai-me-she-kia-kiak or Black Hawk*, 1833) (reprint, Urbana: University of Illinois Press Prairie State Books, 1954, 1990).

Stark, William F., *Along the Black Hawk Trail* (Sheboygan, WI: Zimmerman Press, 1984). [Out of print.]

[No works of interpretation on the Black Hawk War are considered as thorough and as objective as the works on some other wars, although there are several good compilations of primary sources. While noting that no person thanked either endorsed or disparaged any titles, *JIW* acknowledges the assistance of bibliographies or book lists produced by staff members of Illinois State Historical Society; State Historical Society of Wisconsin; Wisconsin Department of Natural Resources. Thanks also to Dave Gjeston.)

6. *Second Seminole War, 1835-1842*

Hartley, William B., *Osceola, the Unconquered Indian* (New York: Hawthorn Books, 1973).

Laumer, Frank, *Dade's Last Command* (Gainesville: University of Florida Press, 1995).

Mahon, John K., *The Second Seminole War, 1835-1842*, rev. ed. (Gainesville: University of Florida Press, 1985).

McReynolds, Edwin C., *The Seminoles* (Norman: University of Oklahoma Press, 1957).

Peters, Virginia B., *The Florida Wars* (Hamden, CT: Archon Books, 1979). [Out of print.]

See also select chapters of:

Bauer, K. Jack, *Zachary Taylor: Soldier, Planter, Statesman of the Old Southwest.* (1985; reprint, Baton Rouge: Louisiana State University Press, 1993)

Covington, James W., *The Seminoles of Florida* (Gainesville: University Press of Florida, 1993).

Eisenhower, John S. D., *Agent of Destiny: Winfield Scott* (1979; reprint, Norman: University of Oklahoma Press, 1999).

Elliott, Charles Winslow, *Winfield Scott, the Soldier and the Man* (1937 reprint, New York: Arno Press, 1979).

Johnson, Timothy D., *Winfield Scott: The Quest for Military Glory* (Lawrence: University Press of Kansas, 1998).

Kieffer, Chester L., *Maligned General: A Biography of General Thomas Jesup* (Novato, CA: Presidio Press, 1979). [Out of print.]

Silver, *Edmund Pendleton Gaines, Frontier General* (Baton Rouge: Louisiana State University Press, 1949). [Out of print.]

Important related books and specialized books:

Procyk, Richard J., *Guns Across the Loxahatchee: An Archaeohistorical Investigation of Seminole War Sites in Florida, with Special Focus on the Battle of Loxahatchee, January 24, 1838* (Melbourne, FL: Florida Historical Society Press, 1999).

Prince, Henry, *Amidst a Storm of Bullets: The Diary of Lt. Henry Prince in Florida, 1836-1843*, edited by Frank Laumer (Tampa, FL: University of Tampa Press, 1998).

[The Hartley biography of Osceola is included partially on the merits of its being the sole lengthily work on the Seminole leader currently in print. Three major works on Winfield Scott are noted, as each possesses unique strengths: Elliott's biography of Scott is the highly detailed, while Eisenhower's and Johnston's are strong on interpretation. While noting that no person thanked either endorsed or disparaged any titles, *JIW* acknowledges the assistance of bibliographies or book lists produced by staff members of Florida State Historical Society and Seminole Wars Historic Foundation. Thanks also to John K. Mahon.]

7. *Wars of the Pacific Northwest, including Cayuse War, 1847-1848; Rogue River Wars, 1853, 1855-1856; Yakima War, 1855-1856; Spokane-Coeur D'Alene War, 1858*

Beckham, Stephen Dow, *Requiem for a People: The Rogue Indians and the Frontiersmen* (1971; reprint, Corvallis: Oregon State University Press, 1996).

Grassley, Ray H., *Indian Wars of the Pacific Northwest*, 2nd ed. (Portland: Binsford & Mort, 1972).

Schlicke, Carl P., *General George Wright: Guardian of the Pacific Coast* (Norman: University of Oklahoma Press, 1988).

Schwartz, E. A., *The Rogue River Indian War and Its Aftermath, 1850-1890* (Norman: University of Oklahoma Press, 1997).

See also specific chapters of:

Potomac Corral of the Westerners, *Great Western Indian Fights* (1960; reprint, New York: MJF Books/Fine Communications, 1997).

Ruby, Robert H., and John A. Brown, *The Spokane Indians: Children of the Sun* (Norman: University of Oklahoma Press, 1970).

Utley, Robert M., *Frontiersmen in Blue: The United States Army and the Indian, 1848-1865* (1967; reprint, Lincoln: University of Nebraska Press, 1981).

Important related and specialized books:

Kip, Lawrence, *Indian War in the Pacific Northwest: The Journal of Lieutenant Lawrence Kip*, with introduction by Clifford E. Trafzer (published as *Army Life on the Pacific: A Journal of the Expedition Against the Northern Indians in the Summer of 1858*, 1859; Lincoln: University of Nebraska Press, 1999).

Manring, Benjamin Franklin, *Conquest of the Coeur d'Alenes, Spokanes and Palouses* (published as *The Conquest of the Coeur d'Alenes, Spokanes and Palouses: The Expeditions of Colonels E. J. Steptoe and George Wright Against the "Northern Indians" in 1858*) (published as *Indian Life on the Pacific*, 1912; reprint, Fairfield, WA: Ye Galleon Press, 1975). [Out of print.]

[While only the latter two wars were directly related to one another, the U.S. Army and later historians have tended to view the conflicts in the Pacific Northwest as a continuous series of events. There have been few publications on the region's wars and Grassley's history is, while brief, the only book to date covering all of them. Only the Rogue River Wars are been studied in any depth. While noting that no person thanked either endorsed or disparaged any titles, *JIW* acknowledges the assistance of bibliographies or book lists produced by staff members of Northwest Interpretive Association; Oregon Historical

Society; Seattle Public Library; Washington State Historical Society; Washington State Parks and Recreation Commission. Thanks also to the Spokane, Washington, Convention and Visitors Bureau.]

8. *Apache Wars, 1861-1886*

The Apache Wars were a series of sporadic conflicts with several different bands of Apaches, primarily the Eastern Chiricahua and White Mountain Apaches. There were three recognizable periods of escalated hostilities. There were a) the "Apache Uprising of 1861-1873," which was at its most intense during "Cochise's War," 1861-1863, and the Tonto Basin Campaign, 1872-1873; b) "Victorio's War," 1879-1880; and c) "Geronimo's War/Resistance," 1882-1884 and 1885-1886.

Debo, Angie, Geronimo *The Man, His Time, His Place* (Norman: University of Oklahoma Press, 1976).

Faulk, Odie, *The Geronimo Campaign* (1969; reprint, New York: Oxford University Press, 1993).

Roberts, David, *Once They Moved Like the Wind: Cochise, Geronimo and the Apache Wars* (New York: Simon & Schuster, 1993).

Sweeney, Edwin R., *Cochise: Chiricahua Apache Chief* (Norman: University of Oklahoma Press, 1991).

———, *Mangas Colorado: Chief of the Chiricahua Apaches* (Norman: University of Oklahoma Press, 1998).

Thrapp, Dan L., *The Conquest of Apacheria* (Norman: University of Oklahoma Press, 1967).

———, *Victorio and the Mimbres Apaches* (Norman: University of Oklahoma Press, 1974, 1980).

Worcester, Donald E., *The Apaches: Eagles of the Southwest* (1979; Norman: University of Oklahoma Press, 1992).

See also specific chapters of:

Leckie, William, *The Buffalo Soldiers: A Narrative of the Negro Cavalry in the West* (Norman: University of Oklahoma Press, 1967).

Important related and specialized books:

Collins, Charles, *Apache Nightmare: The Battle of Cibecue Creek* (Norman: University of Oklahoma Press, 1999).

Thrapp, Dan L., *General Crook and the Sierra Madre Adventure* (Norman: University of Oklahoma Press, 1971, 1972).

Turner, Frederick, ed., *Geronimo: His Own Story*, as told to S. M. Barrett, rev. ed. (New York: Meridian Press, 1996).

[While noting that no person thanked either endorsed or disparaged any titles, *JIW* acknowledges the assistance of bibliographies or book lists produced by staff members of Fort Bowie National Historic Site, Fort Davis National Historic Site; Fort Huachuca Museum; Southwest Parks and Monuments Association. Particular thanks also to the staff of the Fort Lowell Museum of the Arizona Historical Society.]

9. *Dakota War of 1862 (or "Minnesota Sioux Uprising") and Dakota Expeditions of 1863-1864*

Anderson, Gary Clayton, *Little Crow: Spokesman for the Sioux* (St. Paul: Minnesota Historical Society, 1986).

Carley, Kenneth, *The Sioux Uprising of 1862*, 2nd ed. (St. Paul: Minnesota Historical Society, 1976).

Clodfelter, Michael, *The Dakota War: The United States Army Versus the Sioux, 1862-1865* (Jefferson, NC: McFarland & Company, 1998).

Ellis, Richard N., *General Pope and U.S. Indian Policy* (Albuquerque: University of New Mexico Press, 1970).

Jones, Robert H., *The Civil War in the Northwest: Nebraska, Wisconsin, Iowa, Minnesota, and the Dakotas* (Norman: University of Oklahoma Press, 1960).

Oehler, C. M., *The Great Sioux Uprising* (1959; reprint, New York: Da Capo Press, 1997).

Schultz, Duane, *Over the Earth I Come: The Great Sioux Uprising of 1862* (New York: St. Martin's Press, 1992).

See also specific chapters of:

Cozzens, Peter, *General John Pope: A Life for the Nation* (Urbana: University of Illinois Press, 2000).

[The Carley history of the Dakota War of 1862 is brief, and the Oehler and Schultz narratives, though of genuine literary worth, might not be considered military or ethnographic histories. Clodfelter's is the only book to date on the Dakota Expeditions (as well as the Dakota War of 1862); it is concise and is limited in interpretation but is an worthwhile secondary source of information. A guidebook,, *A Traveler's Companion to North Dakota State Historic Site*s, edited by J. Signe Snortland, is also a useful source of facts and maps on the 1863-1864 expeditions (Bismarck: State Historical Society of North Dakota, 1996). While noting that no person thanked either endorsed or disparaged any titles, *JIW* acknowledges the assistance of bibliographies or book lists produced by staff members of Historic Fort Snelling; Minnesota Historical Society; State Historical Society of North Dakota. Thanks also to Vance Nelson.]

10. *Bozeman Trail War or Red Cloud's War, 1867-1868*

Brown, Dee, *The Fetterman Massacre* (printed as *Fort Phil Kearny: An American Saga*, 1962; Lincoln: University of Nebraska Press, 1971).
Keenan, Jerry, *The Wagon Box Fight*, rev. ed. (Eldorado Hills, CA: Savas Publishing Company, 2000).
Larson, Robert W., *Red Cloud: Warrior-Statesman of the Lakota Sioux* (Norman: University of Oklahoma Press, 1997).

See also specific chapters of:

Hyde, George E., *Red Cloud's Folk: A History of the Ogala Sioux Indians*, rev. ed. (1937; reprint, Norman: University of Oklahoma Press, 1967, 1975).
———, *A Sioux Chronicle* (Norman: University of Oklahoma, 1956).
Murray, Robert A., *Military Posts in the Powder River Country of Wyoming, 1865-1894* (1968; reprint, Buffalo, WY: The Office, 1990).
Vaughan, J. W., *Indian Fights: New Facts on Seven Encounters* (Norman: University of Oklahoma Press, 1966). [Out of print.]

Important related and specialized books:

Hagan, Barry, *Exactly in the Right Place: A History of Fort C. F. Smith, Montana Territory, 1866-1868* (El Segundo, CA: Upton and Sons, 1999).

McDermott, John D., *Frontier Crossroads: The History of Fort Caspar and the Upper Platte Crossing* (Caspar, WY: The City of Caspar, 1997).

Tall Bull, Bill, *We Are the Ancestors of Those Yet to Be Born: The Northern Cheyenne Story of the Battle of 100-in-the Hands (the Fetterman Fight)* (Sheridan, WY: Fort Phil Kearny/Bozeman Trail Association, 1988.)

Vaughan, J. W., *The Battle of Platte Bridge* (Norman: University of Oklahoma Press, 1963). [Out of print.]

[Brown's *The Fetterman Massacre* is good popular history, but neither it nor any other work deals with all major facets and locations of the Bozeman Trail War. While noting that no person thanked either endorsed or disparaged any titles, *JIW* acknowledges the assistance of bibliographies or book lists produced by Fort Kearny/Bozeman Trail Association; Frontier Heritage Alliance; Little Bighorn Battlefield National Monument; Wyoming State Museum. Thanks also to Fr. Barry Hagan, Jerry Keenan, and Mary Ellen McWilliams.]

11. *Southern Plains War of 1867-1869 (including Sheridan's Winter Campaign of 1868-1869)*

Berthong, Donald J., *The Southern Cheyennes* (Norman: University of Oklahoma Press, 1963).

Hoig, Stan, *The Battle of the Washita: The Sheridan-Custer Indian Campaign of 1867-1869* (Norman: University of Oklahoma Press, 1967).

Kraft, Louis, *Custer and the Cheyenne: George Armstrong Custer's Winter Campaign on the Southern Plains* (El Segundo, CA: Upton and Sons, 1995).

Monnett, John, *The Battle of Beecher Island and the Indian War of 1867-1869* (Niwot: University Press of Colorado, 1992).

Nye, Wilbur S., *Plains Indian Raiders: The Final Phases of Warfare from the Arkansas to the Red River* (Norman: University of Oklahoma Press, 1968).

See also specific chapters of:

Dixon, David, *Hero of Beecher Island: The Life and Military Career of George A. Forsyth* (Lincoln: University of Nebraska Press, 1994).

Grinnell, George Bird, *The Fighting Cheyennes* (1915; reprint, Norman: University of Oklahoma, 1956).

Hutton, Paul Andrew, *Phil Sheridan and his Army* (1985; reprint, Norman: University of Oklahoma Press, 1999).

King, James T., *War Eagle: A Life of General Eugene A. Carr* (Lincoln: University of Nebraska Press, 1963). [Out of print.]

Leckie, William H., *The Military Conquest of the Southern Plains* (Norman: University of Oklahoma Press, 1963).

Mayhall, Mildred P., *The Kiowas* (Norman: University of Oklahoma Press, 1962).

Utley, Robert M., *Frontier Regulars: The United States Army and the Indian, 1866-1890* (1973; reprint, Lincoln: University of Nebraska Press, 1984).

[While noting that no person thanked either endorsed or disparaged any titles, *JIW* acknowledges the assistance of bibliographies or book lists produced by staff members of Fort Larned National Historic Site; Fort Supply State Historic Site, Oklahoma; Southwest Parks and Monuments Association; Washita Battlefield National Historic Site. Thanks also to Jerome Greene, Stan Hoig, Louis Kraft, and Robert M. Utley.

12. *Red River War, 1874-1875* (not to be confused with Canada's Red River Expedition of 1870)

Chalfant, William Y., *Cheyennes at Dark Water Creek: The Last Fight of the Red River War* (Norman: University of Oklahoma Press, 1997).

Haley, James L., *The Buffalo War: The History of the Red River Indian Uprising of 1874* (1976; reprint, Austin: State House Press, 1998).

See also specific chapters of:

Fehrenbach, T. R., *Comanches: The Destruction of a People* (1974; reprint, New York: Da Capo Press, 1994).

Hagan, William T., *Quanah Parker, Comanche Chief* (Norman: University of Oklahoma Press, 1995).

Hamilton, Allen Lee, *Sentinel of the Southern Plains, 1866-1878: Fort Richardson and the Northwest Texas Frontier* (Fort Worth: Texas Christian University Press, 1988). [Out of print except as a "book on demand" order.]

Hutton, Paul Andrew, *Phil Sheridan and His Army* (1985; reprint, Norman: University of Oklahoma Press, 1999)

Mayhall, Mildred P., *The Kiowas* (Norman: University of Oklahoma Press, 1962).

Neeley, Bill, *The Last Comanche Chief: The Life and Times of Quanah Parker* (New York: John Wiley & Sons, 1996).

Nye, Wilbur S., *Carbine and Lance: The Story of Old Fort Sill* (Norman: University of Oklahoma Press, 1937, 1951).

Pierce, Michael D., *The Most Promising Young Officer: A Life of Ranald Slidell Mackenzie* (Norman: University of Oklahoma Press, 1993).

Robinson, Charles M., *Bad Hand: A Biography of General Ranald S. Mackenzie* (Austin: State House Press, 1993).

Robinson, Charles M., *Satanta: The Life and Death of a War Chief* (Austin: State House Press, 1997, 1998).

Wallace, Ernest Wallace and E. Adamson Hoebel, *The Comanches: Lords of the South Plains* (1952; Norman: University of Oklahoma Press, 1988).

Important related books and specialized books:

Baker, T. Lindsay and Billy R. Harrison, *Adobe Walls: The History and Archeology of the 1874 Trading Post* (College Station: Texas A&M University Press, 1986).

Kavanagh, Thomas, *The Comanches: A History, 1706-1875* (Lincoln: University of Nebraska Press, 1996).

Monnett, John H., *Massacre at Cheyenne Hole: Lieutenant Austin Henely and the Sappa Creek Controversy* (Niwot: University Press of Colorado, 1999).

[Haley's *The Buffalo War* is generally reliable, but the Red River War lacks a definitive history. Incorporation of the information provided by Texas archeological surveys in 1999 and 2000 should greatly aid future works. While noting that no person thanked either endorsed or disparaged any titles, *JIW* acknowledges the assistance of bibliographies or book lists produced by staff members of Fort Sill Museum and the Texas Historical Commission. Thanks also to Brett Cruse, Neil Mangum, and John Monnett.

13. *Great Sioux War of 1876-1877*

Gray, John S., *The Centennial Campaign: The Sioux War of 1876* (1976; reprint, Norman University of Oklahoma Press, 1988).

Greene, Jerome A., *Yellowstone Command: Colonel Nelson A. Miles and the Great Sioux War, 1876-1877* (Lincoln: University of Nebraska Press, 1991.)

Mangum, Neil, *The Battle of the Rosebud: Prelude to the Little Bighorn* (El Segundo, CA: Upton and Sons, 1987).

Robertson, William Glenn, comp., *Atlas of the Sioux Wars* (Fort Leavenworth, KS: Combat Studies Institute,, U.S. Army Command and General Staff College, 1993). [Not available to the public except for use at federal document depository libraries.]

Stewart, Edgar I., *Custer's Luck* (Norman: University of Oklahoma Press, 1955).

Vaughan, J. W., *The Reynolds Campaign on Powder River* (Norman: University of Oklahoma Press, 1961). [Out of print.]

See also specific chapters of:

Hutton, Paul Andrew, *Phil Sheridan and His Army* (1985; reprint, Norman: University of Oklahoma Press, 1999)

Monaghan, Jay, *Custer: The Life of General George Armstrong Custer* (1959; reprint, Lincoln: University of Nebraska Press, 1971).

Sandoz, Mari, *Crazy Horse: The Strange Man of the Oglalas* (1942; reprint, Lincoln: University of Nebraska Press, 1992).

Utley, Robert M., *Cavalier in Buckskin: George Armstrong Custer and the American Military Tradition* (Norman: University of Oklahoma Press, 1991; rev. ed. forthcoming in 2001).

———, *The Lance and the Shield The Life and Times of Sitting Bull* (New York: Henry Holt, 1993).

Vestal, Stanley, *Sitting Bull: Champion of the Sioux,* new ed. (1957; reprint, Norman: University of Oklahoma Press, 1989).

Important related books and specialized books:

Fox, Richard, *Archaeology, History and Custer's Last Battle: The Little Big Horn Reexamined* (Norman: University of Oklahoma Press, 1993)

Gray, John S., *Custer's Last Campaign: Mitch Boyer and the Little Bighorn Reconstructed* (1991; reprint, Lincoln: University of Nebraska Press, 1993)

Greene, Jerome A., ed. and comp., *Battles and Skirmishes of the Great Sioux War, 1876-1877: The Military View* (Norman: University of Oklahoma Press, 1993).

——, ed. and comp., *Lakota and Cheyenne: Indian Views of the Great Sioux War* (1994; reprint, Norman: University of Oklahoma Press, 2000).

——, *Slim Buttes, 1876: An Episode of the Great Sioux War* (Norman: University of Oklahoma Press, 1982).

Hedren, Paul, L., *First Scalp for Custer: The Skirmish at Warbonnet Creek Nebraska, July 17, 1876* (Glendale, CA: Arthur H. Clark Company, 1980). [Out of print.]

——., *Traveler's Guide to the Great Sioux War: The Battlefields, Forts, and Related Sites of America's Greatest Indian War* (Helena: Montana Historical Society Press, 1996).

Michno, Gregory F., *Lakota Noon: The Indian Narrative of Custer's Defeat*, (Missoula, MT: Mountain Press Publishing Company, 1997)

Scott, Douglas, et al., *Archaeological Perspectives on the Battle of the Little Bighorn: The Final Report* (Norman: University of Oklahoma Press, 1989).

Scott, Douglas, et al., *Archaeological Perspectives on the Battle of the Little Bighorn: The Final Report* (Norman University of Oklahoma Press, 1989).

Sklenar, Larry, *To Hell with Honor: Custer and the Little Bighorn* (Norman: University of Oklahoma Press, 2000).

[Many of the books above are in-depth or topical studies. Readers in search of a good concise introduction to the Little Bighorn Campaign are referred to Peter F. Panzeri's *Little Big Horn 1876: Custer's Last Stand* (Mechanicsburg, PA: Stackpole Books, 1995) or Wayne Michael Sarf's *The Little Bighorn Campaign, March-September 1876* (Conshohocken, PA: Combined

Publishing, 2000). Sandoz's *Crazy Horse* and Vestal's *Sitting Bull* have some serious shortcomings in terms of scholarship but remain "classic" works in terms of literary accomplishment. The books above are included because they are widely recognized as works that adhere to high standards of scholarship while remaining comprehensible to readers without extensive previous reading in the subject. *JIW* recognizes that several excellent titles pertinent to the "Great Sioux War" are excluded and is solely responsible for the omissions. Additional works of significance—either secondary works with great breadth or depth of detail or compilations of primary sources—include:

Evans, David C., *Custer's Last Fight: The Battle of the Little Big Horn* (El Segundo, CA: Upton and Sons, 1999).

Greene, Jerome A., *Evidence and the Custer Enigma: A Reconstruction of Indian-Military History* (Reno, NV: Outbooks, 1986).

Hammer, Kenneth, *Custer in '76: Walter Camp's Notes on the Custer Fight*, new ed. (Norman: University of Oklahoma Press, 1990).

Hardorff, Richard, ed. and comp., *Camp, Custer, and the Little Bighorn: A Collection of Walter Mason Camp's Research Papers on General George A. Custer's Last Fight* (El Segundo, CA: Upton and Sons, Publishers, 1997).

——, *Cheyenne Recollections of the Custer Fight* (Glendale, CA: Arthur H. Clark, 1993; paper printing, Lincoln: University of Nebraska Press, 1997).

——, *Lakota Recollections of the Custer Fight* (Lincoln: University of Nebraska Press, 1999).

Hedren, Paul L., *Fort Laramie and the Great Sioux War* (printed as Fort Laramie in 1876: *Chronicle of a Frontier Post at War*, 1995) (Lincoln: University of Nebraska Press, 1998).

Liddic, Bruce R. and Paul Harbaugh, *Camp on Custer: Transcribing the Custer Myth* (Glendale, CA: Arthur H. Clark Company, 1995; reprinted in paper as *Custer and Company: Walter Camp's Notes on the Custer Fight* [Lincoln: University of Nebraska Press, 1998]).

Monaghan, Jay, *Custer: The Life of General George Armstrong Custer* (1959; reprint, Lincoln: University of Nebraska Press, 1971).

Nichols, Ronald H., ed. and comp., *Reno Court of Inquiry: Proceedings of a Court of Inquiry in the Case of Major Marcus A. Reno* (Crow Agency, MT: Custer Battlefield Historical and Museum Association, 1992.)

Rankin, Charles E., ed., *Legacy: New Perspectives on the Battle of the Little Bighorn* (Helena: Montana Historical Society Press, 1996). [Anthology.]

Willert, James, *Little Big Horn Diary: A Chronicle of the 1876 Indian War* (1977; reprint, El Segundo, CA: 1998). [Like the work below, largely a chronology.]

——, *March of the Columns: A Chronicle of the 1876 Indian War: Aftermath of the Custer Battle* (El Segundo, CA: Upton and Sons, 1994).

[We are thankful to the dozens of individuals who provided bibliographies, comments, and information that assisted in compiling this list; many of their names are listed in "Essential Books for Understanding the Battle of the Little Bighorn: Journal of the Indian Wars Asks the Experts" elsewhere in this issue. Particular thanks to Paul Hedren, Michael J. Koury, and James Willert and also to James Court, Neil Mangum, Robert M. Utley and other past and present superintendents and historians of Little Bighorn Battlefield National Monument.]

14. *Nez Perce War, 1877*

Beal, Merrill D., *"I Will Fight No More Forever:" Chief Joseph and the Nez Perce War* (1963; Seattle: University of Washington Press, 1982).

Brown, Mark H., *The Flight of the Nez Perce: A History of the Nez Perce War* (New York: Capricorn Books, 1967; paper printing, Lincoln: University of Nebraska Press, 1967).

Greene, Jerome A., *Nez Perce Summer, 1877: The U.S. Army and the Nee-Me-Poo Crisis* (Helena: Montana Historical Society Press, 2000.)

Important related and specialized books:

Josephy, Alvin M., Jr., *The Nez Perce Indians and the Opening of the Northwest* (1965; reprint, Lincoln: University of Nebraska Press, 1979).

McDermott, John D., *Forlorn Hope: The Battle of White Bird Canyon and the Beginning of the Nez Perce War* (Boise, ID: Idaho State Historical Society, 1978). [Out of print.]

Wilfong, Cheryl, *Following the Nez Perce Trail: A Guide to the Nee-Me-Poo National Historic Trail with Eyewitness Accounts* (Corvallis: Oregon State University Press, 1990).

[The narratives by Beal and Brown are included for their literary quality though Greene's *Nez Perce Summer* is the definitive military history of the war as well as being readable. While noting that no person thanked either endorsed or disparaged any titles, *JIW* acknowledges the assistance of bibliographies or book lists produced by staff members of Nez Perce National Historical Park, including its Big Hole National Battlefield unit; Montana Historical Society; Northwest Interpretive Association. Thanks also to Jerome Greene, Alvin M. Josephy, and John D. "Jack" McDermott.]

15. *"Campaign Against the Northern Cheyennes, 1878-1879" (outbreak and pursuit of Dull Knife's and Little Wolf's bands)*

Monnett, John H., *Tell Them We Are Going Home: The Odyssey of the Northern Cheyennes* (Norman: University of Oklahoma Press, 2001).

Sandoz, Mari, *Cheyenne Autumn* (1953; reprint, Norman: University of Oklahoma Press, 1992).

See also specific chapters of:

Buecker, Thomas R., *Fort Robinson and the American West, 1874-1899* (Lincoln: Nebraska State Historical Society, 1999).

Hoig, Stan, *Fort Reno and the Indian Territory Frontier* (Fayetteville: University of Arkansas Press, 2000).

Utley, Robert M., *Frontier Regulars: The United States Army and the Indian, 1866-1890* (1973; reprint, Lincoln: University of Nebraska Press, 1984).

[Sandoz's *Cheyenne Autumn* is a work of such eloquence that it is included in the list above. However, it contains a number of semi-fictional elements and factual errors that leave it now superseded by Monnett's *Tell Them We Are Going Home*. While noting that no person thanked either endorsed or disparaged any titles, *JIW* acknowledges the assistance of bibliographies or book lists produced by staff members of the Nebraska State Historical Society. Thanks also to John H. Monnett.]

Addenda: Northwest Rebellion of 1885

Morton, Desmond, *The Last War Drum: The North West Campaign of 1885*, Canadian War Museum Historical Publication Number 5 (Toronto: Hakkert, 1972).

Stanley, George F. G., *The Birth of Western Canada: A History of the Riel Rebellions* (1936; Toronto, Buffalo: University of Toronto Press, 1992).

See also secific chapters of:
Dempsey, Hugh A., *Big Bear The End of Freedom* (Vancouver: Douglas & McIntyre, 1984).
Miller, J. R., *Skyscrapers Hide the Heavens: A History of Indian-White Relations in Canada*, 3rd ed. (Toronto: University of Toronto Press, 2000).
——, *Big Bear (Mistahimusqua)* (Toronto, ECW Press, 1996).
Sluman, Norma, *Poundmaker* (Toronto: Ryerson Press, 1967).
Stanley, George F. G., *Louis Riel* (Toronto: Ryerson Press, 1963).
Woodcock, George, *Gabriel Dumont: The Métis Chief and His Lost World* (Edmonton, Hurtig Publishers, 1975).

Important related books and specialized books:

Beal, Bob and Rod Macleod, *Prairie Fire: The 1885 North-West Rebellion* (Edmonton: Hurtig Publishers, 1984).
Bowsfield, Hartwell, comp., *Louis Riel, the Rebel and the Hero* (Toronto: Oxford University Press, 1971).
Dunn, Jack, *The Alberta Field Force of 1885* (Calgary: Jack Dunn Publisher, 1994).
Hildebrandt, Walter, *The Battle of Batoche: British Small Warfare and the Entrenched Métis* (Ottawa: National Historic Parks and Sites, Parks Canada, 1985).
Flanagan, Thomas, *Louis "David" Riel: Prophet of the New World* (Toronto University of Toronto Press, 1979).
——, *Riel and the Rebellion: 1885 Reconsidered* (Saskatoon, Sask.: Western Producer Prairie Books, 1983).
Stonechild, Blair and Bill Waiser, *Loyal Till Death: Indians and the North-West Rebellion* (Calgary: Fifth House Publishers, 1997).

[While noting that no person thanked either endorsed or disparaged any titles, *JIW* acknowledges the assistance of bibliographies or book lists produced by staff members of Batoche National Historic Site (Parks Canada); Battleford National Historical Park (Parks Canada); Center for Canadian Studies at Mount Allison University; National Library of Canada. Thanks also to J. R. Miller.]

INTERVIEW

A Conversation with Historical Novelist Terry Johnston (1947-2001)

Terry C. Johnston of Montana was the most prolific and successful author of historical novels set during Western American Indian conflicts. His Titus Bass or "Mountain Man" trilogy, often praised for its literary quality, is perhaps to general readers his best known series. The premier Bass book, *Carry the Wind*, received the Western Writers of America Pipe Bearer's Award in 1982 for best first novel. Many readers of this journal are also familiar with his "Plainsman" series" of fifteen novels, which proceed through the life of fictional soldier Seamus Donegan. Though these books are admired for their historical accuracy, *Kirkus Review* observed that the "Plainsman novels always offer more than just pulp-style rehashes of American history." Johnston's other novels include both prequel and sequel additions to the original Titus Bass books, a "Sons of the Plains" trilogy about an imaginary son of George Custer by the Cheyenne Monahsetah, and the gritty Jonah Hook trilogy. His last published Plainsman title, *Lay the Mountains Low* (2000), was the second work in which character Donegan takes part in the Nez Perce War of 1877.

The following conversation between Johnston and editor Michael A. Hughes was conducted while touring Texas battlefields of the Red River War (1874-1875) during last year's annual conference of the Order of the Indian Wars.

Terry was diagnosed recently with rapidly advancing colon cancer, and he died shortly before this issue went to the printer. He will be missed at this year's Western Writers, Order of the Indian Wars, and other meetings at which he was a popular figure. Terry's phenomenal commercial success created continuous demands on his time, but he remained notably approachable and down to earth. His wide knowledge, wit, and gift for expression made him wonderful company in private and an eloquent speaker in public. Terry was also well known for the support and generosity he extended to authors, researchers, and history buffs. Some of the information below will be made outdated by his passing. However, *Journal of the Indian Wars* decided to proceed with publication of this interview as a tribute to a good friend and great gentleman of the West.

Johnston's family has provided the names of three appropriate organizations to which contributions might be made in his memory:

1. Terry C. Johnston Memorial Scholarship Fund, Montana State University-Billings Foundation, 1500 North 30th Street, Billings, MT 59101; phone 1-406-657-2244;

2. National Colorectal Cancer Research Alliance, c/o Entertainment Industry Foundation, 11132 Ventura Boulevard, Suite 401, Studio City, CA 91604-3156; phone 1-800-872-3000; donations Web site <nccra.org/how_to_help/.donation.cfm>;

3. Custer Battlefield Preservation Committee, P.O. Box 7, Hardin, MT 59034; phone 1-406-665-1876; fax 406-664-3133; e-mail <custertours@juno.com>. [Donations made to the committee during 2001 will be doubled by an anonymous donor.]

MAH: Should we start with the novel you didn't write, the one about the demon-possessed bear?

TCJ: So you know about that!

MAH: Terry, we're used to thinking of you as a novelist, but you had quite a variety of occupations before you settled into writing, didn't you?

TCJ: Oh yes. I've been a tool pusher on an oil rig, a welder on a pipeline, a dog catcher, a truck driver, and a schoolteacher.

MAH: Where and how were you brought up? Specifically, was there anything in your background that made you especially interested in the history of the West? How did you become a novelist?

TCJ: We spent many years moving around. I was born in 1947 in southeastern Kansas but later lived in Oklahoma, Nebraska, and Arizona, the latter for ten years. My maternal grandmother taught school on the Osage Indian Reservation in northern Oklahoma. Our "family business" has been teaching high school history. In 1967, I was taking a history course at Central State University [Ok]. We didn't have a textbook for it, but were instead reading different books about the early exploration of the Old West. One of these was Bernard DeVoto's *Across the Wide Missouri*. As I read it, a light went on.

I had grown up with Western movies with [character actor] Gabby Hayes types, frontier wagon trains, that sort of thing. Now, Eureka! I discovered the West of the mountain men, the fur traders, the great scouts. I studied all I could about the early frontier for the next seven years. Most of my reading was in rare book rooms of libraries—the university presses didn't have the kind of historic reprints available then that they do now. I graduated college in 1970, then taught school. By 1974, I was no longer teaching because I had a story I really wanted to write about a mountain man. I was out to tell a story though, not write a novel. In fact, I didn't get that story realized until I'd produced three books.

I shared what I was writing with some aficionados of the North American Fur Trade Conference, and several people said I should try to publish my work, that the material was as good as anything currently out there. But I received twenty-nine rejection letters! One publisher who did show an interest wanted me to change the main character to a mountain *woman*. This was when Stephen King's horror novels were taking off and the movie *The Exorcist* was hot. I got another suggestion that I make the main character a possessed grizzly, with my mountain man, Titus Bass, out to redeem himself in battle with the evil bear.

I set the Titus manuscript on the shelf a year and a half. Then a friend of a friend wanted to produce my book as his new company's first fiction publication. This was in 1980, and *Carry the Wind* came out in 1982. We sold a lot of copies by direct mail and by ads for a core audience interested in the West. Bantam Books became interested between the first and second book, and their agent in New York City offered me a three-book contract. Bantam had never tried to sell anything like the original Mountain Man series before 1982. It wasn't about a familiar subject, like cowboys and cattle drives, and they had trouble sticking the work into a cubbyhole. But Bantam launched what has become a four-book series. The third book of the Mountain Man trilogy sequel, *Wind Walker*, will be coming out in April 2001.

MAH: How far along is the Plainsman series about Seamus Donegan and the Indian Wars? [This series follows all of the major Western Indian wars of the latter nineteenth century, beginning with the Bozeman Trail or "Red Cloud's" War (1866-1868), through the adventures of Sergeant Seamus Donegan.]

TCJ: The fifteenth book [*Lay the Mountains Low*], the second about the Nez Perce War, recently came out. There will be twenty-two books in the series, ending with one set at the tragedy at Wounded Knee (1890). Of course, the "Sons of the Plains" or Custer trilogy also deals with the Indian wars.

MAH: How did the character Seamus and his Indian wars series develop?

TCJ: I already had five novels completed before I wrote the first in the series, *Sioux Dawn* [about the 1866 Fetterman "Massacre" and other events at Fort Phil Kearney, Montana]. By then I was being published by two publishers, with two books through Bantam and three through Saint Martin's Press. I had an idea in my head for a new character. After I sent a three-page proposal for a new book, I sent St. Martin's a one-paragraph character sketch. I knew that Seamus would be a former sergeant in the Union army, who would grow up during a quarter century in the West following the Civil War. His personal activities would be subplots in the stories of the campaigns of the Indian wars. Each of twenty-five proposed books would deal with a single campaign, each ending with a story of a battle told from multiple viewpoints. The series would end with Wounded Knee, the last major conflict of the Indian wars.

MAH: How typical do you think that Seamus is of Western novel heroes? How typical of frontier soldiers?

TCJ: The publishers were shocked when they read the prologue to *Sioux Dawn*. The book begins with Seamus being dragged out of a post guardhouse the day before the Fetterman Massacre. They were used to heroes, and Seamus is a sort of antihero. Seamus is also not typical of Irish immigrants in the frontier army. Many of them arrived in their teens while Seamus was already a veteran.

MAH: To what extent are the characters in Plainsman novels fictional?

TCJ: I always work in essential historical figures. Seamus, his wife Samantha, and their son are the only major fictionalized characters. But some of the historical characters in the books are little known, like the bugler at the Battle of Beecher Island (1868) in *The Stalkers*.

MAH: Are the rest of the Plainsman books all that you have projected now?

TCJ: No. There are fifteen other potential novels; I've also agreed to once a year do a biographical novel based on the life of famous mountain men like Jim Bridger, Jebediah Smith, and Jim Beckwourth. This will be the "Pathfinder" series published by St. Martin's in both hard and soft cover. I've also agreed to do a series of stand alone [i.e., non-series] novels on the Astorians [fur trapping party], Sitting Bull, the Alamo, and the Battle of New Orleans (1815). And I'd like to possibly do a trilogy on the Civil War in the [Trans-Mississippi] West.

MAH: Since you started with your interest in the mountain men and the fur trade, how did you become interested in the Indian wars?

TCJ: The wars gradually sucked me in. I've gotten more and more interested in them as I've learned about them. I saw the wars originally as a dichotomy, with the issues simply good versus bad, red versus white. Then I found all of these nuances represented on both sides. I'd been making the same mistake the white government made—seeing the Indians in monolithic terms, with this chief or that their leader. That's why you have the idea of genocide supported from the top down, from [Generals of the Army William T.] Sherman and [Philip H.] Sheridan. But the men and officer at the front regarded the enemy from what we today might call a more "global view." They could see the warriors as family men too. They understood that the Indians were protecting their home. It wouldn't be going too far to say that the soldiers respected them.

MAH: Which battles of the Indian wars particularly fascinate you?

TCJ: Some of the battles in the early years, when a small group of soldiers would be pinned down and realize that "this is likely where we are going to die" and a calm would take over. I'm thinking of battles like the Wagon Box Fight (1867), the Hayfield Fight (1867), and the Fetterman Fight (1866) during Red Cloud's War. I think of Isaac Fisher [at the Fetterman disaster] and his determination to take as many men down with him as he could. Or of Beecher Island (September 17-25, 1868), where they were down to twenty-eight men after the first Cheyenne charge. There you had heroism against devastating odds. The same is true of Roman Nose's [the Cheyenne Woqini's] charge at Beecher Island. Even the scouts' admiration for him comes through. There he makes the decision to fight, knowing he is facing death, because the warriors want him to lead them even though his "medicine" is broken.

But I also admire men like Red Cloud [the Lakota chief Makpiya-luta]. Red Cloud earned a lot of standing legitimately—he had counted a lot of coup—but his position was co-opted for political and personal reasons when he began to compromise with whites. It was Red Cloud who saw what was needed for the Sioux to survive. I'm now working on Crazy Horse's last days (1877). He and Red Cloud had not seen each other since spring of 1867, for ten years. Crazy Horse had stayed what the whites called "wild." He finally came north to the Red Cloud Agency. The two of them had a momentous meeting. Crazy Horse had been the leader of the decoys who had lured [Capt. William J.] Fetterman to his death in Red Cloud's War. Now Red Cloud asked Crazy Horse, "Why do you make so much trouble for the Oglala?" And Crazy Horse asked Red Cloud, "Why didn't you stay out and fight?" They were both disappointed in the other.

MAH: What's the book on Crazy Horse going to be called?

TCJ: *Turn the Stars Upside Down: The Last Days and Tragic Death of Crazy Horse* [projected publication date of August, 2001].

MAH: Who are some of the other people who especially interest you, whom you've written about or would like to write about?

TCJ: Well, there's White Bull, the man known as "Ice." He's in my novels *Wolf Mountain Moon* and *Ashes of Heaven*. He offered himself as a hostage during the negotiations with Nelson Miles after the Battle of Wolf Mountain (1877) and later becomes a scout to help bring in the Northern Cheyenne. Captain Jack [Kintpuash] was a tragic figure. Before the negotiations with General [E. R. S.] Canby [at Lava Beds, California, 1873] he's goaded, called a woman if he won't kill Canby when he meets him. Later, he's the only Modoc War leader to be hanged. There's also Geronimo [Goyathlay]. I'd like to do at least two books on the Apache leaders Victorio [Beduiat] and Geronimo.

On the military side, there's [Maj.] Guy V. Henry. I picture him at the [Battle of the] Rosebud, when he followed [Lt. Col. William] Royall to Royall's third retreat position. Here's one lone officer still on horseback in the middle of it all, instructing his men to turn and fire by volley. He was a conspicuous target, with the Indians only 10-20 yards away. He was shot through the face. In the fight that followed, at least one Shoshone scout stepped over his body to protect it. Then there's Bugler [Adolph] Metzger at the Fetterman Fight, clubbing away with his trumpet when he has nothing else to fight with. Although all the other bodies were mutilated, his was found face to the sky, covered by a buffalo robe as a sign of respect by the Indians for his bravery. That's the sort of people I like to portray—the common heroes. There are a lot of under-appreciated people and events in the Indian wars that deserve attention.

MAH: How much research goes into the "Plainsman" series?

TCJ: There's at least two months worth of research per [military] campaign before I even start writing, though there's far more to study with some than others. Some are hard to get a handle on. The Rosebud fight, for example. I didn't realize that I needed to think of it in terms of three separate battles. The Modoc War (1872-1873), the subject of *Devil's Backbone*, was difficult. There had been so little on it for general readers when I started to research it.

MAH: I know you like to see the places you're writing about before you describe them in your novels. Does that sometimes change what you write? Are there times you're gotten what you thought was an accurate impression from books and then found that the reality was different when you saw a location?

TCJ: Well, yes. I remember the first time I saw the Wheatley-Fisher Rocks near where Fetterman was killed. That's where [James] Wheatley and [Isaac] Fisher held off what must have seemed a small army of Cheyenne and Lakota with the Henries [Henry repeating rifles]. I'd always read, or at least expected, that the rocks were huge boulders that the men would have been safe behind. When I actually saw them, it didn't seem as if I was in the right place. The rocks were much smaller than I expected, providing a lot less cover. The Rosebud Battlefield (1876) is another example. You really have to see that battlefield to understand the great scale of the battle.

MAH: Could we pause for a "commercial" here? You have a very good record for supporting Indian wars battlefield preservation groups. I know that a percentage of the profits from several of your ventures have gone into that. Why do you think it's important that the western battlefields be protected?

TCJ: Well, as I sort of suggested when I talked about Wheatley-Fisher Rocks, there are some events you can't understand unless you can actually see and walk on the location. Another case would be the place where they fought the

Hayfield Fight. I didn't understand how exposed and vulnerable the soldiers there were until I saw the place. By the way, the actual site of the [hayfield] corral is at least three-fourths of a mile from where the 1933 monument is. It's on private land and could be obliterated by construction. At least you can make a copy of a book or manuscript. But you have to be more careful with land. Anyone owning a battlefield is in a position of trust. Once the battlefield is altered, the record is lost. There is a lot of information we would be without if we didn't have the place to examine, especially when there aren't documentary records. Information on the Fetterman Fight, which had no survivors, is a good example of this. You can't tell what happened there if you can't go there.

That's why the Custer Battlefield Preservation Committee [preserving the Little Bighorn Battlefield] is so important. The Little Bighorn Battlefield is on an interstate highway, it's owned by a variety landowners, and it's vulnerable to development. Right now we have the best—and maybe the only—opportunity to save it. I admire all of the people fighting lonely battles to protect the battlefields. Some of those "gatekeepers of history" are ranching families who love their land and appreciate its significance. I'm thinking of the Smarts at Summit Springs [Battlefield, 1869] and Cheri Grove at the Dull Knife Battlefield [1876]. I believe she's charging $75 for visits now and she has a right to it—she really looks after that land, and it's hard to keep a ranch going today.

MAH: You've told me several times how indebted you are to historians. Who are some of them whose work has been most helpful?

TCJ: There's [Dee] Brown, [Fred] Werner, and [Fairfax] Downey. And there are the professional historians, like [Neil] Mangum, Jerry [Jerome A.] Greene, and John McDermott, and of course Bob Utley. Greene's work has helped me immensely. Were it not for a photocopy of his work in progress on the Nez Perce or Nee-Mee-Poo War, I couldn't have written *Cries from the Earth*. [Greene's *Nez Perce Summer* was published in 2000 by the Montana Historical Society Press.] I tell everyone that I'm a "pickpocket" of academic historians. Their books are my tools, and my toolbox is getting large and expensive! Some of them are very good writers too. I wish Paul Hutton would write more. He makes wonderful use of language; it's very engaging.

MAH: How have historians reacted to your novels?

TCJ: They've usually been well received. [Paul Andrew] Hutton and Bob Utley have both commented on their accuracy. Utley did me the honor of saying that if ever I lived a previous life, it was as a mountain man.

MAH What do you think distinguishes the way you write from the way that historians write, other than yours being fiction versus non-fiction.

TCJ: Actually, I lean heavily on the non-fiction to write what I do. However, there is a difference in my having a story to tell. I start with some element that will grab the reader, and with each chapter I draw the reader farther into the story. Also, historians, at least academic historians, usually write longitudinally. I love to jump back and forth in the narrative and also to make events move more quickly at times. When I close my eyes, I can see the action on the back of my eyelids like a motion picture.

MAH: You keep saying you learn a lot from historians. Is there anything the average writer of history could learn from a novelist?

TCJ: Probably how important it is to be descriptive. A lot of histories are not vivid enough.

MAH: I've heard you describe yourself as an author of historical novels set in the West, rather than an author of "Westerns." Why the distinction?

TCJ: When I started to write, in the '70s, the great traditional Western writers—like Will Henry—were almost gone. Louis L'Amour was the only thing close to a Western writer left. A lot of what's been passing for "Westerns" is just pulp fiction that could be set in any time and place. The real focus of some of it is violence and sex—some of what's out there is very anti-women. Fortunately, the market for things like that seems to be shrinking. There's a lack of research in that kind of "Western," and that's a great injustice to the genre. The same is true even of some "historical novels" set in the West. The "history" only comes in when it's convenient. Of course, the other extreme is work that's historically accurate but not good fiction.

MAH: So who are some of the other legitimate "authors of historical novels set in the West?" Whose work do you especially like?

TCJ: I owe a lot to Will Henry (whose real name was Clay Fisher) and Douglas C. Jones. I usually don't read fiction other than "real" fiction.

MAH: That's interesting, because it seems as if your books have made a lot of your readers more interested in history.

TCJ: There is a great body of readers not interested in the Indian wars who wouldn't have picked up a book on them if it hadn't been fiction. Now, after reading the novels, they hopefully know more about them. They know more than just a few famous names. And since they're reading a series, they can see each war as part of a epic contest for the West, especially in the ten or more years before and after the [Battle of] the Little Bighorn (1876).

MAH: Terry, thanks. Thanks for the interview, and thanks for what you're done to encourage interest in history and in historic preservation.

TCJ: My pleasure. Thank you for your interest in my books.

Terry Johnston's "Plainsman" series novels and their battles:

Sioux Dawn (Fetterman Massacre, 1866).
Red Cloud's Revenge (Wagon Box Fight and Hayfield Fight, 1867).
The Stalkers (Beecher Island, 1868).
Black Sun (Summit Springs, 1869).
Devil's Backbone (battles of the Modoc War, 1872-1873).
Shadow Riders (battles of the Southern Plains Uprising of 1873).
Dying Thunder (battles of the Red River War, Second Adobe Walls to Palo Duro Canyon, 1874-1875).
Blood Song (Reynolds's Battle of Powder River, 1876).
Reap the Whirlwind (Rosebud Creek, 1876).
Trumpet on the Land (Slim Buttes, 1876).
A Cold Day in Hell (Dull Knife Battle/South Fork of Powder River, 1876).
Wolf Mountain Moon (Battle of the Butte/Wolf Mountain, 1877).
Ashes of Heaven (battles of the conclusion of the Great Sioux War, including Lame Deer, 1877).
Cries From the Earth (opening battles of the Nez Perce War, including White Bird Canyon, 1877).
Lay the Mountains Down (continuing battles of the Nez Perce War, including Big Hole, 1877).

The Indian Wars

Battlefield, Tribal, Preservation, and Museum News

Queen Anne's War: Mission San Luis and the Apalachee Indians. In the seventeenth century, the Apalachee were a significant factor in the settlement of the current southeastern United States. Their "revolt" in 1647 was one of the most serious acts of defiance against eastern Indian incorporation into the empire of Spain. However, the Apalachee became integral to Spanish plans for church and imperial control of North America. Mission San Luis de Apalachee was the de facto western capital of Florida from 1656 to 1704. Recognizing the community's importance, the English twice attempted to destroy San Luis during Queen Anne's War (1702-1713). In 1704, English leaders and a large group of their Lower Muskogee ("Creek") allies forced the evacuation of the mission town and destroyed it.

The excavated community is now the site of a Florida state historical park on the outskirts of Tallahassee. The state and an extremely active local support group have been reconstructing some of the most important structures. During the past two years, archaeologists and volunteers have recreated the Indian council house and the mission church. According to site historian John H. Hann, the next task will be locating the line of, and reconstructing, one face of the central defensive stockade. The volunteers of Mission San Luis and the Museum of Florida History produce several news periodicals concerning their projects, including *El Correo* and *The Quarterly* (Mission San Luis de Apalachee, 2020 W. Mission Road, Tallahassee FL 32304). The state's Web site on San Luis at <dhr.dos.state.fl.us/bar/san_luis/index.html>. (Source: John H. Hann; Volunteers of Mission San Luis and the Museum of Florida History.)

Wars in the Old Northwest/"Little Turtle's War:" Blue Jacket (Weyapiersenwah) was one of the most important Shawnee leaders of Indian resistance to the loss of Indian land. An increasing number of scholars are now convinced that he was the driving force in the last phases of the so-called "Little Turtle's War" (1790-94) against the young Untied States republic. Somehow, a rumor has persisted for generations that Blue Jacket was actually a white man, specifically one Marmaduke Van Swearingen. The story is mentioned in Allan W. Eckert's biography of Blue Jacket. In the words of Robert Denton Blue Jacket, a descendent living in Oklahoma, "The white man has always relished the idea that the great chief Blue Jacket was actually their white chief." In 2000, a Wright State University [Ohio] biologist was able to compare DNA samples of five living members of the Van Swearingen and Blue Jacket families. The results provide strong evidence that that Blue Jacket was an Indian. (Source: Old Northwest Historical Society.)

In Volume One, No. 2 of *JIW*, archaeologist J. Michael Pratt described the climactic battle of Little Turtle's War, the Battle of Fallen Timbers, Ohio (August 20, 1794). At that time we noted the drive to make the 1794 battleground an affiliated unit of the United States's National Park Service. Congress authorized the creation of a national historic site incorporating Fallen Timbers and Fort Miamis [sic] in late 1999. *JIW* is pleased to report that federal funds were authorized for land acquisition in October, 2000, in part through the efforts of Ohio congresswoman Marcy Kaptur. The 185-acre battlefield will be owned and managed by Toledo Metroparks. The state of Ohio, city of Maumee, and Fallen Timbers Battlefield Preservation Commission are currently reimbursing the city of Toledo, Ohio, $5.5 million. Toledo had purchased the land as an investment before the discovery that it, rather than a previously preserved area, was the battlefield. Fallen Timbers Community Church deserves special recognition. Members raised an $8,000 donation for the battlefield by creating and charging admission to an autumn "corn maze" shaped like the face of General Anthony Wayne.

Indian Removal/Trail of Tears. Ironically, an Illinois-based railroad company is attempting to drive the citizens of the United States away from the route over which the country once drove away its Indians. (See below.) The compulsory emigration of eastern United States Indian nations to reservations west of the Mississippi River caused violent friction between the plains and prairie tribes already there and the newcomers. In 1817, Fort Smith, Arkansas, was established on the eastern edge of the [Oklahoma] Indian Territory. It was to preserve peace between the Osage and the relocated Cherokee and to serve as part of the so-called "permanent Indian frontier." The army largely abandoned the post in 1824 as the "permanent" frontier moved west but returned and began construction of a new Fort Smith in 1839. However, most people associate Fort Smith with the fact that the famed "Hanging Judge" Isaac C. Parker and his marshals presided over the U.S. Court of the region when the military handed over the buildings to judicial authorities.

For many years the limited interpretation at Fort Smith National Historic Site seemed to focus in large part on the structures' last role, that of courthouse and jail. This changed dramatically with the reopening of the remodeled visitor center in the Barracks/Courthouse building in June 2000. The number of exhibits and audiovisual programs has enormously expanded, as has the amount of history interpreted. There is considerably more coverage of the military's role in Western expansion and peacekeeping than previously. Fort Smith is also a unit of Trail of Tears National Historic Site, which commemorates the removal of the Cherokee and other nations. This is finally evident in the far greater emphasis on Indian history in the new visitor center. In addition, a walking stop and overlook at the nearby Arkansas River commemorates the Trail of Tears. This overlook was designed in conjunction with the "Five Civilized Tribes" which were removed to Indian Territory and was dedicated jointly with them in August 2000.

Unfortunately, land access to the overlook and over half of the acreage of the national historic site may soon be impossible. The federal land is bisected by two railroad lines. One of these lines, used for excursions, has a handicapped accessible crossing. The other crossing, that of the Fort Smith Railroad (owned by an Illinois corporation) does not. The Fort Smith Railroad maintained a foot crossing over its tracks from the 1960s, and for decades did not interfere with public access to the western half of the national historic site. In 2000, however, a citizen complained to the railroad and the National Park Service that the railroad's crossing did not comply with the Americans with Disabilities Act. Shortly afterwards, the railroad company tore out the pedestrian crossing and announced that it would fence off its right of way through the national historic site. All other access is already blocked by construction and the Arkansas River. The Fort Smith Railroad's action will prevent citizens and park authorities from visiting the western half of their national historic site.

This western section contains the largest concentration of physical landmarks of the Trail of Tears and Indian Removal. These include the visible foundations of the first Fort Smith, the initial point for the survey of the Indian

Territory, and the moorings of the Choctaw ferry on the main water route for Indian removal. The National Park Service and the sympathetic city government of Fort Smith are currently exploring their options with regard to the railroad's actions. *JIW* will try to keep readers informed about the crisis.

Second Seminole War. The Seminole Wars Historic Foundation has been for the past three years increasingly active in research and historic preservation concerning the Seminole Wars. Their achievements include the reprinting of Woodburne Potter's 1836 *The War in Florida* and and the editing and publication of Lieutenant Henry Prince's war journal. (See this issue's book reviews.) The non-profit organization has also acquired options to purchase the site of Fort Dade, used as a security outpost and negotiation site, and the important Fort Izard/"Gaines's Battle"/Withalacoochee battleground (1836). The latter is proving a rich archaeological site. Honorary foundation council memberships of $25 earn the donator honorary ownership of one square foot of one of the two sites. For more information on the foundation, contact Seminole Wars Historic Foundation Inc., 35247 Reynolds Avenue, Dade City, FL 33523; phone (352) 583-2974.

Second Seminole War: The Battle of Lake Okeechobee (1837) was the turning point in what was, in terms of the commitment of funds and troops, the largest Indian war in the Americas. The engagement is occasionally described as one of the few won by both sides: the Seminoles dropped their more serious attacks, and many agreed to emigrate, yet the United States lost its revolve to totally remove them from Florida. Unfortunately, much of the battlefield faces the likelihood of residential construction. This situation is complicated by the fact that new historical and archaeological research has led to a rethinking of the battle's probable location. For several years the National Park Service has listed the site as an "at risk" National Historic Landmark. The unrelated National Trust for Historic Preservation has designated Okeechobee as one of "America's 11 Most Endangered Historic Places." (On the Internet, see <www.nationaltrust.org/11most/okee.htm>.) In the fall of 2000, the American Battlefield Protection Program of the National Park Service announced the granting of $35,000 to the Archaeological and Historical Conservancy for an Okeechobee Battlefield archaeological survey. The conservancy is to "determine the locations of all significant battlefield components and develop a battlefield land acquisition plan." The contact for information is Robert S. Carr,

Executive Director, Archaeological and Historical Conservancy, Inc., 111 SW5th Avenue, Suite 302, Miami, FL 33130; phone (305) 325-0789. The National Trust recommends that citizens concerned about the future of the battlefield express their views by writing Governor Jeb Bush, The Capital, Tallahassee, FL 32399-0001 or by e-mailing Governor Bush at <fl_governor@eog.state.fl.us>.

Sand Creek Massacre, 1864—A bill to create Sand Creek Massacre National Historic Site was approved by the U.S. Senate in late 2000, shortly after the November 29 anniversary of the engagement. Colorado volunteer troops led by Colonel John M. Chivington killed an estimated 150 to 200 Southern Cheyenne and Arapaho on Sand Creek despite the belief of Chief Black Kettle that those encamped were protected by an informal armistice. The bill seeks to authorize the creation of a 12,480-acre memorial at the eastern Colorado site, provided the ranch family who currently own the location will sell willingly. *JIW* described the archaeological discovery of the massacre site in issue I,3. Our next issue will feature an interview with National Park Service researcher Jerome Greene in which he discusses the clues that led to the discovery.

Paiute War (1866-1868), Battle of Infernal Caverns. The Paiute War in California and Oregon is little known today other than for the striking name of this September 1867 battle and the fact that the conflict set George Crook on his rise to prominence as an Indian wars general. (The conflicts is sometimes referred to by the ambiguous term "Snake War.") The Sierra Pacific Power Company is running a power line across Bureau of Land Management (BLM) land in the general vicinity of, though not across, the battleground. Because the line will cross federal land, the company has agreed to pay mitigation costs that can be used to fund the development of trail and interpretive facilities on or near the battlefield. The actual battlefield is on private property and is not accessible to the public, though BLM is trying to negotiate access for the public. (For this reason, *JIW* cannot and will not provide any access directions at this time.) BLM officials have provided *JIW* with a projected schedule for development: "An updated plan for the area will be completed by 9/30/2001. Complete archaeological/T&E inventories on the trails and facilities will be conducted by 9/30/2002. Mitigation for cultural resources will be complete by 9/30/2003. Trail construction, facilities, and interpretive displays will be in place by

9/30/2005. The proposed schedule ... and project completion is partially based on present funding, and additional funding needs." Any information that readers have that might be useful in the interpretation of the "Infernal Caverns story" would be appreciated by BLM. The contacts are Tim Burke (Field Manager) or Claude Singleton, Bureau of Land Management, Alturas Field Office, 708 West 12th, Alturas, CA 96101; phone (530) 233-4666.

Sioux War of 1876-1877 and Battle of Marias River (1870). The Frontier Alliance's study and action plan for six battlefields of the 1876 campaigns of General George Crook has been completed. The study was funded by a $21,600 grant from the American Battlefield Protection Program of the [United States] National Park Service. In addition, over $12,000 worth of in-kind service were donated by a variety of interested organizations and individuals. The grant recipient, the Frontier Alliance, is a coalition of agencies, Indian tribes, educational institutions, and landowners working for the preservation, interpretation, and economic development of the Northern Plains. The project's supervisor, historian and advisor John D. McDermott, identified some of the goals as providing information on the battles, bringing in the Indian side of the battle stories, encouraging public-private cooperation to preserve the battlefield, and assisting in the preparation of a cultural resource management plan for Montana's Rosebud Battlefield State Park. McDermott notes that twenty-five copies of the 1,100 page study are being provided to key organizations and archives.

In the fall of 2000, the Frontier Alliance also received $36,000 from the American Battlefield Protection Program for the "Baker's Battlefield Documentation Project." The Alliance will conduct, with the consent of the Lakota Nation (which now controls access to the northern Montana battlefield), an archaeological survey of the site and the adjacent Tracy's Steamboat Landing. Hopefully, the study will produce a National Historic Landmark nomination for the battleground; the location is currently indefinite. Major Eugene Baker's attack on a village of Piegan "Blackfoot" Indians in January 1870 was a controversial event in which as many as 173 Indians were killed. The surprisingly little-known event is sometimes referred to even by army defenders as the "Baker Massacre" or "Marias [River] Massacre." For more information, contact Howard Boggess, Frontier Heritage Alliance, 1004 Big Goose Road, Sheridan, WY 82801; phone (406) 656-9961.

Nez Perce War, 1877—*Nez Perce Country*, the official handbook for Nez Perce National Historic Park, is an excellent concise guide to the "Nez Perce" or Nee-Mee-Poo Indian nation and the course of its war of resistance and flight in 1877. The book is listed as "out of print" and "out of stock" by all sources. However, a small number of copies have been located and may be obtained by specific request from the Northwest Interpretive Association. Contact Nez Perce National Historical Park, Attn: Northwest Interpretive Association, Route 1, Box 100, Spalding, ID 83540; phone (208) 843-2261, extension 124. Copies of the handbook are $15.95 each. Postage and handling are an additional $2.00 for the first item and $1.00 each additional item, to a maximum of $6.00. Orders may be placed by telephone using a valid credit card. The Northwest Interpretive Association, one of several "cooperative groups" aiding the national parks, carries all other significant titles on the Nez Perce War. Members of other national park associations, such as Eastern and the Southwest Parks and Monuments Association, may receive a reciprocal discount on purchases.

Western History Association. The Western History Association sponsored its first military history luncheon at the October 2000 annual conference in San Antonio. Among the organizations represented at the informal luncheon were CAMP (below) and *Journal of the Indian Wars*. The W.H.A. fall, 2001, conference will be held in San Diego, California. The theme for the meeting will be "The American West as Living Space." For additional information, contact Western History Association, University of New Mexico, 1080 Mea Vista Hall, Albuquerque, NM 87131-1181; phone (505) 277-5234.

CAMP Conference—May 2001. The Council on America's Military Past (CAMP) hosted its 35th Annual Military History Conference in and around Rapid City, South Dakota, on May 9-13, 2001. Topics of the thirty papers presented ranged from the American Revolution, Civil War, and Indian wars to the Vietnam War and the Cold War era. (*JIW* associate editor Rodney G. Thomas was one of the speakers.) Additional information on this conference and the next one, as well as CAMP membership ($35 individual subscribing) may be obtained from CAMP, P.O. Box 1151, Fort Myer, VA 22210; phone (703) 912-6124; fax 703-012-5996; or e-mail <camphart1@aol.com>.

Custer on the Plains Tour. Action Travel and Custer Tours are offering an intensive autumn tour of six days' travel to Custer and other sites on the plains of Kansas and Oklahoma. Overnight October 14, 2001, in Kansas City, then spend six days traveling to sites including Fort Leavenworth, Beecher's Island and Summit Springs, Washita Battlefield National Historic Site, and Fort Larned National Historic Sites. The cost is $1,100 (double occupancy). *JIW* does not normally promote commercial activities; however, this tour will be led by Little Bighorn Battlefield superintendent Neil Mangum and Custer Battlefield Preservation Committee chairman Jim Court, both of whom have been very generous in their support of historical research and preservation. For more information, contact Action Travel, Box 310, Hardin, MT 59034; custertours@juno.com; phone (406) 665-1580.

Battle of the Little Bighorn 150th Anniversary Events

Editor's note: The multitude of names used below may seem confusing but all of the terms refer to the same battle, an engagement involving three battalions of the Seventh Cavalry Regiment. The Battle of the Little Bighorn took place in three separate phases and locations. These were a) the initial fight by Marcus Reno's battalion at "Reno's Valley Battlefield" in the Little Bighorn River valley; b) the siege of Reno and Frederick Benteen's combined battalions at the "Reno-Benteen Battlefield" atop the river's bluffs, and; c) the fight of the battalion led by George Custer personally ("Custer's Last Stand") on the "Custer Battlefield" on Custer Ridge. The federal land at the separate Reno-Benteen and Custer battlefields constitutes what is today known as Little Bighorn Battlefield National Monument. This national monument was formerly known as "Custer Battlefield National Monument." "Big Horn" is an alternate and perhaps older rendering of the name of the river.

June 26-27, 2001, mark the 150th anniversary of what is likely the most famous Indian wars engagement in North American History, the 1876 Battle of the Little Bighorn or Greasy Grass. The city of Hardin, Montana's "Hardin Little Big Horn Days" (June 21-25) is a well-known annual event that includes the Custer's Last Stand Reenactment. The reenactment typically involves nearly 300 participants, attracting more than 10,000 viewers during the course of four performances. This year's performances (June 22-24) are expected to receive international attention. In addition, the National Park Service and several Indian wars groups are planning a number of special ceremonies and educational events this year for Little Bighorn Battlefield National Monument. Unfortunately, the battle anniversary has created an unavoidable scheduling conflict for four of the excellent organizations described below. Hotels and campgrounds in southeastern Montana and northeastern Wyoming are expected to be filled to capacity from June 20 through May 28. Anyone wishing to see the battlefield during the period is advised to make reservations for accommodations well in advance and to expect difficulties in visiting the national monument.

For information on Little Big Horn Days, contact Hardin Chamber of Commerce, 15 East 4, Hardin, MT 59034. Tickets for the Custer's Last Stand Reenactment may be purchased online at www.mcn.net/!custerfight/ or by phone from (888) 450-3577.

Custer Battlefield Preservation Committee—An anonymous donor has offered to match all donations made to the Custer Battlefield Preservation Committee during 2001. Donations of $500 or more will be double matched. *JIW* has several times previously publicized the efforts of the committee. Currently Little Bighorn Battlefield National Monument contains and protects only a fraction of the total acreage of the land involved in the battle. The non-profit Preservation Committee independently protects several land holdings near the entrance to the battlefield from commercial development. Currently the committee is attempting to purchase the site of Sitting Bull's Lakota village and the unprotected "Reno's Valley Battlefield." The group has also been approached about purchasing the Medicine Tail Coulee crossing, a significant feature involved in George Custer's movements. Donations for the cause may be made by check or by credit card. To make donations, get information, or arrange private battlefield tours, write CBPC, Box 7, Hardin, MT 59034, or phone chairman Jim Court at Action Travel at (406) 665-1876.

A year 2001 calendar featuring photographs of Deer Medicine Rocks on Rosebud Creek, the location of the vision quest in which Sitting Bull received his revelation of "soldiers falling into camp" prior to the battle, is now available for $15. A portion of the proceeds will go to the preservation committee. For calendars, write Kim Donel, P.O. Box 225, Lewistown, MT 59457 (e-mail kdphoto@mcn.net).

Little Bighorn Battlefield National Monument Symposium and Ceremonies, June 25-26—Ceremonies included a June 25 reading of the names of all known warriors and soldiers who died on the field, and a joint wreath laying at the Seventh Cavalry Monument and site of the future Indian Memorial. A June 26 symposium (with Friends of Little Bighorn), "Remembering Little Bighorn," was held in nearby Hardin, Montana. For information on all events at Little Bighorn Battlefield, contact Superintendent, Little Bighorn Battlefield National Monument, P.O. Box 39, Exit 510 Off K-90 Hwy 212, Crow Agency, MT 59022-0039; phone (406) 638-2621.

Custer Battlefield Historical & Museum Association Annual Meeting, June 21-24, Hardin, Montana—The Plains war research and Little Bighorn Battlefield advocacy group concentrated on events scheduled around Little Bighorn Battlefield National Monument. The activities included a living history encampment, a field trip to the battlefield, special ceremonies, a memorial service at the national monument, and a June 22 symposium. For information on membership ($15 annual U.S. membership; $25 non-U.S.) or meetings, contact CBHMA, P.O. Box 902, Hardin, MT 59034-0902; phone (406) 665-2060.

Little Big Horn Associates Conference, June 21-23, Sheridan, Wyoming—The 28th national conference of LBHA was held on June 22, and included an intensive tour of the battlefield. For more information on future events, contact Bill Serritella, Treasurer LBHA, P.O. Box 1160, LaGrange Park, IL 60526-1160.

Order of the Indian Wars Assembly, June 21-24, Sheridan, Wyoming—OIW held its 23rd annual assembly of the Order of the Indian Wars at the Best Western Sheridan Center. Speakers included Tom Bullhead (grandson of the Lakota policeman who shot Sitting Bull), anthropologist Margot Liberty, *JIW* editor Michael Hughes, author Jerry Keenan, and military historian Peter Panzeri. For information on the meeting or membership ($20 annual) contact Jerry Russell/OIW, Box 7401, Little Rock, AR 72217 or visit the OIW web site (http://www.indianwars.com/).

BOOK REVIEWS

Digging Into Custer's Last Stand, by Sandy Barnard with "Battle Overview" by Brian Pohanka. (AST Press, 1998. Pp. 164. Photographs, charts, maps. Paper, $10.00; cloth $24.95.)

They Died with Custer, by Douglas D. Scott, P. Willey, and Melissa Connor. (Norman: University of Oklahoma Press, 1998. Pp. 389. Contents, photographs, charts, bibliography, index. Cloth $29.95.)

Digging into Custer's Last Stand is for this reviewer "the one that got away." Many years earlier, Sandy Barnard approached my firm, Old Army Press, with the predecessor to this current fine effort. I told Sandy the book was too long and contained far too many personal anecdotes. What I wanted, I told him, was a shorter book, with more details on the "finds" rather than on the "finders." As it turns out, Sandy was right though, in the way of saving face, I can claim the honor of bringing his AST Press into being. Sandy decided to publish the manuscript himself and has since published several other outstanding works under the AST imprint.

Digging Into Custer's Last Stand give the reader an insider's look at virtually every important archaeological event at Little Bighorn Battlefield, Montana, since the 1983 fire that fortuitously provided an excuse to begin investigation the next year. The book covers the digs of 1985, 1989, and 1994 within the boundaries of the national monument as well as the excavation done before reconstruction of the Custer home at Fort Abraham Lincoln, North Dakota. A last minute addition discusses the remarkable finds made by Jason Pitsch on the site of Major Marcus Reno's skirmish line, which was outside the current boundaries of the monument. It was the latter finds that led to the creation of the short-live but spectacular Reno Museum that was placed squarely on Reno's line in the Little Bighorn valley.

The knowledge gained from the 1984 through 1994 digs has greatly enlarged our knowledge of George Armstrong Custer's defeat on June 25, 1876. Unfortunately, the information gained has only increased the controversy over the course of the engagement, rather than diminished it. After examining all of the new information, dig director Doug Scott, supervisory archaeologist for the National Park Service Midwest Archeological Center (Lincoln, Nebraska), concluded that a "last stand" likely did occur at Custer's final position. Scott also felt the dig offered convincing proof that the solders held their ground wherever they fought in Custer's sector of the battlefield. "My feeling is, based on the artifact pattern, that the men must have fairly well held their positions," he remarked. However, archaeologist Richard Fox, Doug's second-in-command and an extremely knowledgeable interpreter in his own right, came to an opposite conclusion. Fox wrote a well-received book, *Archaeology, History and Custer's Last Battle* (1993) that viewed much of the battle as a series of collapses and routs. Both men used the same excavations as the basis for their conclusions. So much for science nailing down definitive answers.

Having served as media director for the 1985 and 1989 archaeological projects, as well as for the 1986 human remains reburial service, Sandy Barnard is uniquely qualified to write this book. It is his "inside" take that makes the book more interesting to the average reader than the heavier tomes published by Scott, et al. Sandy's personal insights and his perhaps more detached view provide the reader with a wealth of information as well as an appreciation for the magnitude of the task of excavation. In addition to being well written, the book is copiously illustrated. All in all, this is a terrific book. The lack of an index and a good bibliography hinder its use slightly, but this can be easily overlooked in view of the outstanding contribution it makes.

They Died with Custer, the most recent book of the above mentioned Scott, is an absolutely invaluable addition to any Custer library. The first third of the book provides a capsule summary of the history of the Seventh Cavalry that alone would have provided justification for the title's publication. This regimental history is followed by a company-by-company analysis of the regiment after the Battle of the Little Bighorn.

Scott, Willey, and Connor's analysis puts to rest beyond questions the attempt to ascribe Custer's defeat to heavy numbers of raw recruits in his ranks at the battle. A look at the officers shows that 61 percent had Civil War experience and 40 percent were West Point graduates. Only three of the forty-three officers had less than one year's active army service. Similarly, a majority of the enlisted men and non-commissioned officers were veterans. The authors provide statistics such as these percentages for each individual company. They establish the conclusion that the Seventh Cavalry was an experienced regiment by the standards of its day.

Rather than merely providing statistics, *They Died with Custer* shows the value of multi disciplinary historical analysis. The amount of information that can be obtained from a tooth or a finger bone staggers the imagination. The book provides the reader with a detailed look at life on the frontier, particularly as regards the U.S. Army, as revealed by the combination of skeletal remains and military records. The soldiers' food, use of tobacco, dental condition, size, and ethnic origin are all examined. One surprising revelation from the investigation is that the average weight of members of the Seventh Cavalry was slightly greater than that of the populace at large. Other surprises abound.

The books also describes the traditional location of the identified dead on the battlefield, along with reported alternate locations. Facial reconstructions from skull bones give an educated guess as to the identities of several previously unidentified remains. A full account is presented of the various reburials of remains. The squeamish may wish to pass by the chapter describing the latter—the details of the stages of decomposition and the difficulty posed by handling the remains are graphic.

Giving life to bones—a possibility that did not exist before modern forensic science—can greatly increase our understanding of events like Custer's last battle. This amazing book leads the way.

Michael J. Koury, Old Army Press

The Iroquois in the Civil War: From Battlefield to Reservation, by Laurence M. Hauptman. The Iroquois and Their Neighbors Series. (Syracuse, NY: Syracuse University Press, 1993. Pp. 214. Contents, preface, introduction, illustrations, charts, maps, notes, bibliography, index. Paper, $19.95.)

The inclusion of studies on the roles of Indians during the American Civil War into the historiographical mainstream is a relatively recent phenomenon. Most of the earlier works on this topic focused on affairs in the Indian Territory and the American West. Laurence Hauptman's *The Iroquois in the Civil War:*

From Battlefield to Reservation breaks new ground. It is a study of one of the great Indian confederations and the role it played in the conflict. In addition to providing a well-researched and superbly written examination of battlefield exploits, the book is a compendium of a people separated onto reservations in Wisconsin and the Indian Territory and the story of the Iroquois from native Northeastern homelands who were also relegated to reservations. Hauptman pays particular attention to the life of perhaps the most famous Iroquois who fought in the war, Ely S. Parker, who was General U.S. Grant's military secretary. The author includes information about the principal Iroquois tribes (Mohawk, Oneida, Onondaga, Cayuga, Seneca, and Tuscarora) and the effects upon them of hardships such as the reduction of population through casualties and the unscrupulous dealings of governmental officials. The effects of the war upon women and children are examined in these same contexts.

Hauptman expertly blends the stories of individuals, military units, geography, and technology into his work. He describes where and under what circumstances the Iroquois entered into service in the Union army and how they were integrated into the force structure. Various campaigns in which they participated are described, including those in the Carolinas and Chattanooga, the Red River Campaign, and Sherman's March to the Sea. There is also a chapter-length study of how technology, particularly railroads, changed the Iroquois during and after the war.

The author uses his last chapter to describe the war's consequences for the Iroquois. He makes a strong case that the Iroquois fought two wars: one on the battlefield and another at home. In the Indian Territory these were often blended into one. The Iroquois had to contend with the fact that their traditional ways, already altered by reservation life, were forever changed by the war. Many of their men were casualties, and those who returned had to fight for their veterans' rights into the twentieth century. Many tribal lands, particularly in New York, were in danger of legal confiscation. Additionally, assimilation into white culture was an almost irreversible trend that continues to this day. Comparisons can be made between the South and the Iroquois in how the Reconstruction and post-Reconstruction eras treated these two groups. As a whole, Southerners fared better.

The book contains excellent maps that aid the reader, perhaps more than is usual. The maps describe the original Iroquois homelands in the Northeast and the locations of reservations in the Northeast, Midwest, and the Indian Territory. There are also campaign maps. The author has also included several photographs of some of his subjects. This book is part of a series called "The Iroquois and Their Neighbors." There are at least twenty volumes in this series, and they cover a broad interdisciplinary approach in the study of the Iroquois. The author is the series editor.

Gary Joiner Louisiana State University, Shreveport

Members of the Regiment: Army Officers' Wives on the Western Frontier, 1865-1890, by Michele J. Nacy. Contributions in American History Series, Number 187. (Westport, CN: Greenwood Press, 2000. Pp. ix, 128. Contents, introduction, endnotes, appendices, bibliographic essay, bibliography, index. Cloth, $55.00.)

Volume 187 in Greenwood Press's Contributions in American History Series, *Members of the Regiment*, is subtitled *Army Officers' Wives on the Western Frontier, 1865-1890*. Michele J. Nacy employs the growing discipline of women's history to examine the lives of these officers' wives and uses the letters and diaries of eleven such women as her main sources. She examines the ways these women lived, their activities both inside and outside the garrison, their attitudes (as far as can be determined) regarding groups such as enlisted men and Indians, and their impact on the army as a whole. Relying on a combination of old and new sources, Nacy brings us a fresh look at an often overlooked side of the frontier army experience.

Given the rising interest in areas such as women's history and minority studies, Nacy's look at the lives of officers' wives is quite timely. Unfortunately, the book appears to have suffered from poor editing. There are a number of factual errors that work to undermine the air of authority that Nacy brings to her subject. For example, George Crook is incorrectly cited as the officer who ordered offensive action from Fort Phil Kearny in 1866 (it was in fact Philip St. George Cooke), and the regiment stationed there is once misidentified as the Eighth Infantry (pages 26 and 17). But perhaps the oddest error comes whenever the narrative turns to Margaret Carrington, the first wife of Colonel Henry Carrington. Not only is the first Mrs. Carrington not included in the book's index, but for some reason her first name is given as "Martha" throughout the text (pages 17, 40 [although here it is applied to Francis Grummond], and 63). Additional confusion also occurs in the chapter titled

"Enlisted Men, Blacks and Mexicans." In this chapter, Nacy discusses the problems many officers' wives had with post quartermasters, even though most such quartermasters were officers and not enlisted men.

It might also have been interesting if Nacy had included the backgrounds of some of the husbands. For example, the two officers' wives she holds up as being most atypical, Alice Baldwin and Alice Grierson, were both married to officers who earned their Regular Army commissions through volunteer service in the Civil War. Mrs. Grierson in particular is worthy of mention, as she married Benjamin before he attained military rank. The non-traditional origins of their husbands and the persecution that both men later suspected on the part of West Point graduates might have had an impact on their wives.

Problems with editing aside, *Members of the Regiment* provides an interesting examination of the writings of some officers' wives and a reasonably balanced assessment of their lives and roles within the traditionally masculine army. Nacy concludes that these women were often quite different from their eastern contemporaries. As "members of the regiment," they found opportunities and obstacles that were foreign to their contemporaries and often had different opinions about issues such as temperance. Perhaps the most interesting portions of the book come from the letters of Ada Adams Vodges. The only unpublished (and thus unedited) set of letters used in *Members of the Regiment*, Vodges' comments are the most candid.

While the price may be a bit rich for the blood of some, *Members of the Regiment* is a useful addition to the bookshelf of anyone researching the frontier army. It gives an authoritative voice to a segment of that army that has long gone unheard.

William Van Horn, Bozeman, Montana

The Great Frontier War: Britain, France, and the Imperial Struggle for North America, 1607-1755, by William R. Nester. (Westport, CN: Praeger, 2000. Pp. xiii, 326. Contents, introduction, bibliography, index. Cloth, $69.95.)

The First Global War: Britain, France, and the Fate of North America, 1756-1775, by William R. Nester. (Westport, CN: Praeger, 2000. Pp. ix, 308. Contents, introduction, bibliography, index. Cloth, $69.95.)

One of the most obvious and confusing problems with William R. Nester's narrative on the "Great War for Empire" in North America is that it is divided between two volumes. The first volume ends in late 1755 when the French and Indian War had been underway for almost two years, and the second volume begins in 1756 when the conflict spread beyond North America and became a global conflagration. For this reason, neither book stands well on its own, and the reader cannot read one of the volumes without reading the other. As Nester's introduction to the first volume makes clear, this was done intentionally. Given the fact that the two books dovetail so closely, it would have been far wiser to produce them as a single volume, or, at the very least, as two volumes under a single title.

The title of the first volume is deceptive because Nester discusses the first four imperial wars in a mere twenty-six pages. The remainder of the first chapter and all of the next two are devoted to an examination of the causes of the French and Indian War as well as the various nations, both European and Indian, that participated in the conflict. Chapters 2 and 3 are definitely the best sections of this volume because Nester provides very useful and highly readable descriptions of the social structures, governments, armies, and navies of Britain, France, the North American colonies, and American Indian communities. The last two chapters of the first volume and all seven chapters of the second volume are broken down chronologically. Chapters 4 and 5 of the first book narrate the events of 1754 and 1755 when the conflict was restricted to North America. Each year from 1756 to 1760 is treated as a separate chapter in the second book, while the events from 1761 to 1776 are covered in the final two chapters. In the second volume, Nester examines global events in places such as Europe, the West Indies, and South Asia, but the focus remains on the war in North America. What is disturbing, however, is that an explanation of how these far-flung battles related to one another and to the greater conflict is largely absent. Nester simply provides isolated narratives of various facets of the confrontation but fails to provide a larger context that serves to illustrate how these events were parts of a larger whole.

There are several other technical problems that further plague these two volumes. First, both are peppered with misspellings and grammatical errors. In the first volume, for example, "Loudoun" is spelled as "Loudon," (20) and the word "sent" is used when "send" was intended (194). In the second volume, "Jacques" is written as "Jacque," (16), "for" is written as "or" (138), and the sentence "Lodging and food was free" appears rather than the grammatically correct "Lodging and food were free" (127). Second, there are several overly long and awkward passages such as that on page 119 of the second volume where Nester quotes directly from other secondary sources. All of this material should simply have been paraphrased.

William R. Nester has produced two volumes that examine the wars of empire fought between France and Great Britain for control of North America. This would be an ambitious project for any historian, particularly since luminaries such as Francis Parkman, Lawrence Henry Gipson, and Francis Jennings have written interpretively significant works that chronicle the imperial struggle for the continent. In the introduction to *The Great Frontier War*, Nester states that the purpose of the first volume is to explore "the events and forces leading up to the [French and Indian] war and its first two years of combat," while the second volume examines the "global war whose carnage mounted until the 1763 treaty ended it." (x-xi) He achieves the goal that he sets forth in the first volume but not the second, and while Nester synthesizes an impressive number of secondary works and published primary sources, he does not say anything new in either volume. There are also several other flaws that detract from the overall quality of these two books. simply have been paraphrased. Third, students of the Indian wars will wince when they read blatantly ethnocentric descriptions of Native American warfare such as "With their blood lust satiated" on page 234 of the first book and "a frenzy of bloodlust" on page 147 of the second volume. Finally, neither book contains any maps, diagrams, or illustrations. The lack of maps is particularly annoying when detailed troop movements are discussed. There are certain strengths to both books. Battles are described in exacting detail, and Nester does an excellent job illustrating the personalities, strengths, weaknesses, competencies, and incompetencies of the major political figures and military commanders. However, these strengths are simply not enough to overcome the numerous mistakes and defects that burden these two volumes.

Patrick J. Jung, Book Review Editor, *Journal of the Indian Wars*

Upton and Sons Proudly Introduces "The Battle of the Little Big Horn" Series

Custer's Last Fight: The Battle of the Little Big Horn, by David C. Evans. Vol. 1 in the new "Battle of the Little Big Horn" series. Evans has synthesized the voluminous LBH literature and arrived at provocative conclusions that will give pause even to the most seasoned Custer student. Excellent maps, original photography, and extensive appendices. 604pp. Photos, notes, index, bibliography, rosters, official documents, maps. ISBN 0-912783-30-3. $85.00. Limited (50 copies) Signed / Numbered Leather Edition: $350.00

Winner of the Little Big Horn Associates "John M. Carroll Best Book Literary Award."

Papers of Edward S. Curtis Relating to Custer's Last Battle, by James S. Hutchins, ed. Vol. 2 in the new "Battle of the Little Big Horn" series. Curtis, a well known photographer, interviewed Custer's Crow scouts and others. The result is this remarkable study, which has never been completely published in book form. Includes a photographic essay "Letting the Photos Speak," by James S. Brust, with "then and now" photos. Robert Utley says, "Hutchins furthers his distinction by presenting new source material on that endlessly debated battle. This contribution to history belongs on every bookshelf." 175 oversize pages, fold-out map, biblio., index. ISBN 0-912783-29-X. $75.00. Limited (50 copies) Signed and Numbered Leather Edition: $275.00

Battle of the Little Big Horn: A Comprehensive Study, by Jack Pennington. Vol. 3 in the "Battle of the Little Big Horn" series. An in-depth examination of the statements and testimony offered by participants of both sides (including more than two dozen Sioux and Cheyenne accounts) and writers who have theorized on the battle. Of special interest is Pennington's critical analysis of the writings of fourteen leading Custer experts. Fresh, controversial, and original. Oversize, 373 pp., maps, photos, biblio., index. ISBN 0-912783-34-6. $85.00. Limited (50 copies) Signed and Numbered Leather Edition: $200.00

UPTON AND SONS, PUBLISHERS
917 Hillcrest Street, El Segundo, California 90245
Web Site: www.uptonbooks.com / E-Mail: richardupton@worldnet.att.net
FREE CATALOG / ORDER: 800-959-1876 / Fax: 310-322-4739

A Classic Indian Wars Title . . .
Completely Revised and Back in Print!

The Wagon Box Fight
An Episode of Red Cloud's War

by Jerry Keenan

ISBN: 1-882810-87-2. Three maps, 27 photos and illus,12 charts, 168pp. Paper only, $14.95, plus $3.30 first class shipping.

Quantity discounts of this and other titles are available. Inquire as to details.

One of the best known Indian battles of the post Civil War West, the Wagon Box Fight has long attracted the interest of writers and students of the Indian Wars. This engagement, in which thirty-two defenders, armed with a newly arrived breech-loading rifle, held off scores of Indian attackers, was the army's response to the tragic Fetterman disaster.

In addition to a complete description of the engagement, this *completely revised* collector's edition features an introduction to the development of the Bozeman Trail, the creation of Fort Phil Kearny, and the events leading up to the Wagon Box Fight. Also included are appendices containing official army reports of the principal officers, as well as a section on the archaeological field work at the site completed by the state of Wyoming.

About the Author: Jerry Keenan is recognized as one of the leading experts in Indian wars history working today. In addition to articles and book reviews, he is the author of the recent *Encyclopedia of American Indian Wars, 1492-1890* (ABC-CLIO, 1999), and a member of the Editorial Advisory Board for *Journal of the Indian Wars*.

Civil War Regiments

A Journal of the American Civil War

If you enjoyed JIW, you will love CWR...

The Battle of the Wilderness:
Grant & Lee Below the Rapidan

A stellar collection! "The Battle of the Wilderness and its Place in the Civil War," by Gordon C. Rhea; "Thomas Stevenson's Division on the Brock Road," by Christopher L. Kolakowski; "Colonel Clark Moulton and the 33rd North Carolina Infantry," by W. Keith Alexander; "The Death, Retrieval, and Remembrance of Brig. General. James Wadsworth," by Eric Mink; "The Battles of Brig. Gen. John M. Jones," by Melissa Delcour; "Plashes and Ambushes: Irish Antecedents in the Wildernes," Kelly J. O'Grady; "Preserving the Wilderness Battlefield," by Mike Stevens. Book reviews, index. 208pp, maps, photos. Paper. ISBN 1-882810-59-7. Vol. 6, No. 4. $12.00.

Gettysburg: Regimental Leadership and Command

"The 35th Battalion Virginia Cavalry," by John Chapman; "Charles W. Reed and the 9th Massachusetts (Bigelow's) Battery," by Eric Campbell; "The Ground Trembled as They Came: The 1st West Virginia Cavalry," by Steve Cunningham and Beth White; "Twice Lost: The 8th Louisiana's Battle Flag at Gettysburg," by Terry Jones; "Major John Nevin and the 93rd Pennsylvania Infantry," by Dana Shoaf; "The Reunion of the Philadelphia Brigade and Pickett's Division, July 1887," by D. Scott Hartwig; "The Continuing Battle," by Walter Powell. Book reviews, index, 208pp. Maps, photos, paper. ISBN 1-882810-57-0. $12.00

The Maryland Campaign
and its Aftermath

The second Antietam issue: "A German Volunteer in the Army of the Potomac," by Anders Henriksson; "Layfayette McLaws' Aide-de-Camp in Maryland," by Helen Trimpi, ed.; "The 79th New York Highlanders," by Terry Johnston; "Battle for Burnside's Bridge," by Keith Toney; "The 118th PA Inf. at Shepherdstown," by Mark Snell; "The Civilians of Sharpsburg," by Ted Alexander; "The Lost Order and the Press," by Scott Sherlock. Book reviews, index. 208pp, maps, photos. Paper. ISBN 1-882810-56-2. Vol. 6, No. 2. $12.00.

North Carolina:
The Final Battles

Focuses on the final actions in the Tarheel State. Includes: "The 26th Wisconsin Infantry in the Carolinas"; The 1st USCT; The Fighting at Town Creek and the Demise of Wilmington; a pair of unpublished Confederates reports from Bentonville; Stoneman's Carolinas Raid, an exclusive interview with historian Craig Symonds, book reviews and index. 188pp. Maps, photos. ISBN 1-882810-54-6. Paper. Vol. 6, No. 1. $12.00.

Most back Issues are available. Write or call for a listing of all our issues.
Please specify Volume and Issue number when placing your order.

Savas Publishing Company
Box 4527, El Dorado Hills, CA 95762 / Voice: 916-941-6896 / email: militarybooks@onemain.com

SATISFY YOUR CRAVING FOR SOMETHING NEW!

Back issues of Journal of the Indian Wars

The premier issue! Custer at the Washita and Little Bighorn: Custer's controversial post-Civil War career is dissected by several authors. Also includes an archaeological essay on the Washita, book reviews, index. ISBN 1-882810-79-1, maps, 18 photos and illustrations. Paper, 144pp. $11.95

Battles and Leaders East of the Mississippi: A number of in-depth articles on Andrew Jackson's battles of Emuckfaw and Enotochopco and Horseshoe Bend; Wayne's 1794 Campaign; Fallen Timbers; the Black Hawk War; and the Indian War in the Old Northwest, plus an iterview, book reviews, index. 188pp., maps, photos, paper. ISBN: 1-882810-80-5. $11.95

The Indian Wars' Civil War: Includes two articles on the Dakota War of 1862, Stand Watie and Ely Parker The Battles of First and Second Cabin Creek, Western American Indian experiences during the Civil War plus an interview, book reviews, and index. 188pp maps, photos, paper. ISBN: 1-882810-81-3. $11.95

Battles and Leaders East of the Mississippi: Andrew Jackson at the battles of Emuckfaw and Enotochopco, and Horseshoe Bend; Anthony Wayne's 1794 Campaign, the Battle of Fallen Timbers; the Black Hawk War Reconsidered; and Secretary of War Henry Knox and the Indian War in the Old Northwest, 1790-1795. Plus, Capt Albert Barnitz's lost account of Washita, an interview with Archaeologist G. Michael Pratt, book reviews, and index. 188pp. maps, photos, paper. ISBN: 1-882810-80-5. $11.95

Savas Publishing Company
P.O. Box 4527, El Dorado Hills, CA 9576
916-941-6896 (phone); militarybooks@onemain.com (E-mail)
www.savaspublishing.com (online web site

Distributed to the trade by Stackpole Books: 800-732-366